Heretics of the Harvest Moon

The True Story of the Witch Trials

W.J. Brendle Ph.D.

BEYOND
THE FRAY PUBLISHING

Copyright © 2025 by W.J. Brendle, Ph.D.
Published by Beyond The Fray Publishing

All rights reserved.
No part of this book may be reproduced in any form or by any electronic or mechanical means, including information storage and retrieval systems, without written permission from the author, except for the use of brief quotations in a book review.

ISBN 13: 979-8-89234-146-2

Full cover created by L. Douglas Hogan

Printed in the USA

Beyond The Fray Publishing, a division of Beyond The Fray, LLC, San Diego, CA
www.beyondthefraypublishing.com

CONTENTS

Preface   v

1. The Origins of Witchcraft and Persecution   1
2. The Rise of Witch-Hunters and Inquisitors   9
3. The Tests and Tortures of Witch Trials   17
4. Kramer, Sprenger, and the Malleus Maleficarum   33
5. Matthew Hopkins is the Witchfinder General   41
6. Scherer, Remy, and Witch-Hunting Hysteria   49
7. Pierre de Lancre and Balthasar von Dernbach   59
8. Michaelis and Caddell in the Witch-Hunt Era   69
9. The Magistrate and the Chief Justice   81
10. Accused Turned into Accusers   91
11. The Witch-Hunting Machine in Europe   99
12. Witch-Hunting in England and Scotland   111
13. Fear and Hysteria in Colonial America   121
14. Witch-Hunts Beyond Europe and the New World   131
15. Stories of Injustice and Courage   147
16. Urban Grandier and the Ursuline Nuns   165
17. Legacies of the Persecuted   179
18. The Decline of Witch-Hunts   191
19. Legacy of Witch-Hunters and the Hunted   213
20. Lessons from Witch Hunts for Today's World   223
     Epilogue   233

Bibliography   235
About the Author   237
Also by W.J. Brendle Ph.D.   239

PREFACE

In history's darkest moments, fear and ignorance have often conspired to bring about the persecution of innocents. Few periods in history are as chilling as the witch-hunts that spanned Europe and parts of the Americas from the 15th to 18th centuries. For hundreds of years, authorities tried, tortured, and often executed ordinary men, women, and even children for the crime of "witchcraft." This term became synonymous with heresy, evil, and rebellion against the accepted social order. But how did societies come to believe that witches were real, dangerous, and in need of elimination? And why were the accusations and persecutions so widespread, affecting not only a few isolated communities but entire nations?

At the heart of the witch-hunt phenomenon lies a complex intersection of social, religious, and political forces. Witchcraft had existed in folklore long before the formal trials began, associated with both benign magick and malicious sorcery. Many ancient societies viewed practitioners of magick as healers or seers, intermediaries with spiritual realms. However, during the late medieval and early modern periods, several cultural shifts fueled a drastic re-evaluation of these beliefs. Christianity, with its view of magick as an offense against God, dramatically altered how people perceived witchcraft. A growing fear of Satanic influence and the conviction that witches were agents of the Devil helped lay the foundation for widespread persecution.

Compounding these religious beliefs was social tensions, economic hardship, and political instability. As communities grappled with famine, disease, war, and social disruption, they sought explanations and scapegoats. Witchcraft, with its associations of hidden malice and supernatural influence, became a straightforward answer. Both religious and secular authorities believed that organized groups of witches plotted against society, and these conspiracies demanded constant suppression. Witch-hunting became a powerful tool for restoring order, often reinforcing authority and control over the population.

This period also produced infamous figures known as witch-hunters, men and women who took it upon themselves to root out suspected witches. Religious or governmental authorities appointed some, while others claimed their role independently, exploiting local fears for personal gain. These witch-hunters developed brutal methods of identifying, interrogating, and condemning those accused. They used gruesome techniques like pricking, swimming, and torture to extract confessions, often focusing their efforts on the most vulnerable members of society. Figures like Matthew Hopkins, Heinrich Kramer, and Christian Caddell became notorious for their relentless campaigns, leaving a trail of death and despair in their wake.

Alongside the infamous witch-hunters were the tragic stories of the accused, men, women, and sometimes even children, whose trials became infamous for their cruelty. Cases such as the

Pendle Witch Trials in England, the Würzburg and Bamberg trials in Germany, and the Salem Witch Trials in colonial America reveal the devastating impact of hysteria. And show how deeply the fear of witchcraft penetrated society. Sometimes, personal vendettas fueled accusations of witchcraft. In other cases, accusers targeted people who lived on the fringes of society or those who acted or behaved in ways that didn't fit societal standards.

In this book, we will explore the witch-hunt phenomenon from multiple angles. Chapter by chapter, we will trace the origins of the belief in witches and the rise of persecution. We'll examine the lives and practices of famous witch-hunters and delve into the infamous trials that stand out in history. We will investigate the methods used to identify witches, including torture and "witch-pricking," and we will explore the theological and legal underpinnings that gave these hunts legitimacy. Finally, we will look at the stories of some of the most notable accused witches, examining the personal tragedies and the broader societal effects of these trials.

Through this exploration, we will uncover the roots of fear and prejudice that fueled these hunts. We will study the cultural, political, and religious contexts that allowed witch-hunting to persist for centuries. This journey into the past will reveal not only the horrors of persecution but also the resilience of those who, even in the face of death, maintained their innocence.

The legacy of the witch-hunts and the witch-hunters is not just one of history. This period of mass hysteria offers enduring lessons about the dangers of unchecked authority. The power of belief, and the consequences of fear to override compassion and reason. Even in modern times, societies still fall prey to similar patterns of persecution and scapegoating. By remembering and

PREFACE

understanding the history of the witch-hunts, we gain insight into the mechanisms of fear and control and perhaps an opportunity to prevent them from recurring.

I dedicate this book to the memory of those who lost their lives and to the continuing struggle against the ignorance and fear that fueled these horrors. As you read, may you find not only the chilling details of the witch-hunters' methods but also the resilient spirit of those who suffered unjustly. A reminder of the courage that can arise even in the darkest of times.

CHAPTER I
THE ORIGINS OF WITCHCRAFT AND PERSECUTION

The belief in witchcraft has its roots in ancient civilizations, going back thousands of years, where magick and mysticism were an integral part of daily life. Ancient societies often viewed magick as a natural force, a tool that those with special knowledge or spiritual power could wield. In this context, people considered witches, or their equivalents in various cultures, to be healers, shamans, and wise individuals. For instance, the ancient Egyptians believed knowledgeable individuals could influence supernatural forces through spells and rituals, many of which were recorded in the famous *Book of the Dead*. People saw magick as a fundamental part of their world, used to heal the sick, protect the dead, or seek guidance from the gods.

In Mesopotamian culture, magick was a versatile tool, employed for a variety of purposes that ranged from protective rituals to healing practices. However, this seemingly benign view of magick coexisted with a growing apprehension towards malevolent forms of sorcery. This dichotomy gave rise to the concept of the witch, a figure associated with the harmful use of magick. The emergence of this figure was not an isolated phenomenon but intertwined with the belief in the malicious application of magick. Magick was thought to be used for causing harm and for promoting good.

In the ancient Babylonian society, the accusation of practicing malevolent magick was a serious matter that could lead to formal trials. This is striking when considering that priests and other religious figures often engaged in magick for protective purposes. A protective spell could possibly cause harm to another individual and be considered malevolent. Knowing how accusations of malevolent magick could still implicate these respected individuals underscores how seriously Babylonian society treated such allegations.

The *Code of Hammurabi*, one of the earliest known legal codes, explicitly addressed cases of sorcery. This legal intervention serves as a notable example of an early attempt to regulate and respond to "witchcraft" accusations. Including such laws in the *Code of Hammurabi* suggests that sorcery and witchcraft were significant issues in Babylonian society. Warranting formal legal responses and contributing to the shaping of societal perceptions and treatment of suspected witches and sorcerers.

The ancient Greeks and Romans had a more complex view. People widely practiced magick and tolerated it as part of the religious and social landscape, but they increasingly suspected its potential to do harm. The Greek goddess Hekate, associated with witchcraft, the moon, and the underworld, embodied the dual nature of magick, both feared and revered. Greek literature, such as Homer's *Odyssey*, presents figures like Circe and Medea, who could manipulate the natural world and transform others. However, these figures often symbolized the dangerous and morally ambiguous aspects of magick. Roman authorities, concerned about harmful sorcery, began sporadic legal persecution during Emperor Augustus's reign. This view would later underpin more intense anti-witchcraft sentiments in medieval Europe.

The *Book of Enoch* introduced concepts of forbidden knowledge and supernatural beings that heavily influenced early Jewish and Christian demonology. In *1 Enoch*, a group of rebellious angels, called the Watchers, descends to Earth and becomes entangled with humanity. This narrative describes how these angels, led by figures like Samyaza and Azazel, teach humans forbidden arts and secrets. This included various forms of magick, weapon-making, astrology, and the use of cosmetics. The corrupting influence of these teachings, known as the "hidden mysteries," leads humans into sin and disobedience, according to God.

This notion of forbidden knowledge, specifically knowledge imparted by fallen angels, laid a conceptual foundation for later Christian ideas about magick and sorcery. Early Christian theologians interpreted the actions of the Watchers as examples of divine boundaries being crossed, with magick representing humanity's attempt to access powers and knowledge meant to be off-limits. As a result, theologians often saw practices like sorcery and divination as inherently connected to demonic influence. This perspective deeply influenced later Christian views, particularly during the Middle Ages, when magick and witchcraft were increasingly associated with dealings with Satan.

Early Christians, some of whom regarded the *Book of Enoch* as authoritative, drew on its themes to develop their demonology. For instance, Azazel, one leader of the Watchers, taught humans how to create weapons and other items that could be used for harm. Azazel's role in the *Book of Enoch* solidified the idea that such knowledge was not only dangerous but morally corrupting, and its usage might symbolize allegiance to evil forces. This association directly contributed to the latter idea that witches possessed dangerous, forbidden knowledge gained through demonic pacts or influences.

In *1 Enoch*, God ultimately judged these fallen angels for their actions, bound and cast them into darkness as punishment. This imagery, which parallels the *New Testament's* depiction of Satan and his demons, reinforced the belief that magickal practices were an affront to divine order. Specifically, the connection between fallen angels and human sin created a theological position where those practicing magick are not only sinners but also active collaborators with evil forces.

The *Book of Enoch* thus introduced a framework to view sorcery and witchcraft not as mere superstition or neutral folklore, but as transgressions aligned with demonic rebellion. When witch-hunts later intensified in Europe, the cultural memory of texts like *Enoch*, which depicted supernatural beings corrupting humankind with forbidden secrets, helped to justify persecution. This cast witchcraft as an inversion of divine will, portraying those accused of practicing it as agents of Satan.

The *Book of Enoch* was influential in early Christian thought regarding forbidden knowledge and heresy. Early Church Fathers such as Tertullian, Origen, and Irenaeus referred to *1 Enoch*. Which they saw as supporting the idea that humans who delved into arcane practices were tampering with the sacred mysteries forbidden by God. This notion of forbidden knowledge was foundational to the church's later view that practitioners of magick, or witches, were knowingly or unknowingly serving the Devil.

The association of forbidden knowledge with heresy also laid the groundwork for the medieval Inquisition. Initially established to root out heretical beliefs, the Inquisition would eventually apply its efforts to suspected witches, whose practices were inherently heretical and, by extension, anti-Christian. Early Christian perspectives on heresy and the corrupting force of forbidden knowledge, influenced by the *Book of Enoch*, contributed to this theological environment. One where those practicing witchcraft are not just individuals breaking social norms but are conspirators in a spiritual battle against God.

The removal of the *Book of Enoch* from the Biblical canon in most Christian traditions occurred long before the medieval witch-hunts. However, their themes lingered in theological and cultural beliefs about sorcery, forbidden knowledge, and demonic influence. These ideas fed into the belief that those practicing witchcraft were not simply superstitious or misguided but were engaged in a dangerous and immoral alliance with evil forces. Thus, the influence of the *Book of Enoch* helped create the paranoia which characterized the witch-hunts in the late medieval and early modern periods.

The *Book of Enoch* contributed to the ideological framework that justified the persecution of witches. The idea humans could access "forbidden" secrets imparted by fallen beings aligned with Satanic pact beliefs that dominated the witch trials. By this logic, witches were not only individuals engaging in illicit practices but traitors to God's order, deserving of the harshest punishments.

As Christianity spread throughout the Roman Empire and later into Europe, its views on magick and sorcery transformed. Early Christian teachings condemned idolatry, paganism, and the use of magick, framing these practices as incompatible with Christian faith. In the *Bible*, several passages reflect this condemnation. The *Old Testament* includes specific prohibitions against witchcraft; for instance, Exodus 22:18 famously states, "You shall not permit a sorceress (witch) to live." A command that would later become a grim justification for executing alleged witches in Christian Europe. Deuteronomy 18:10-12 forbids practices such as sacrifices, divination, interpreting omens, and necromancy, all of which were linked to non-Christian beliefs and rituals.

The early Christian Church emphasized a strict opposition to magickal practices, viewing them as both sinful and spiritually dangerous. As Christianity continued to spread, it encountered existing pagan religions that practiced forms of folk magick and held beliefs in nature spirits and deities. Missionaries often condemned these beliefs as "pagan" and associated them with Satanic influence, a theological stance that laid the groundwork for later accusations of witchcraft. However, in early Christianity, the church primarily sought conversion, not persecution, in its approach to magickal practices. The church sought to replace these beliefs with Christian doctrine, reframing indigenous practices as superstition rather than heresy.

This attitude changed dramatically around the 10th and 11th centuries as the church's power grew, especially in Europe. Christianity's growing emphasis on orthodoxy led to an increased intolerance for beliefs or practices that did not align with church doctrine. Magick, once broadly tolerated as part of folk culture, came to be viewed as heresy, a direct challenge to the church's spiritual authority. Church scholars developed an ideology that branded all forms of "pagan" magick as Satanic in origin, a belief that culminated in a more systematic persecution of those associated with witchcraft.

During the medieval period, the church launched several campaigns to root out heretical beliefs, seeing them as threats not only to individuals but to the stability of Christendom itself. The Cathar and Waldensian heresies, which emphasized unorthodox religious practices, were among the earliest targets of these campaigns. Accusations of witchcraft intertwined with heresy as church authorities sought to eliminate any challenge to religious orthodoxy. In 1233, Pope Gregory IX established the Inquisition, initially aimed at rooting out heretical sects in southern France. Although the early Inquisition did not specifically target witchcraft, it laid the institutional and ideological foundation for later witch-hunts.

The association between witchcraft and Satanism solidified over the 14th and 15th centuries as fears of demonic influence grew. The church and secular authorities alike viewed witchcraft not merely as individual acts of sorcery but as evidence of an organized, Satanic conspiracy aimed at undermining Christian society. A broader cultural fear of Satan and the notion that witches made pacts with the Devil influenced this shift in perspective, using magick to serve his purposes. Texts like *Malleus Maleficarum*, written by Heinrich Kramer and Jacob Sprenger in 1487, further cemented these beliefs by providing guidelines for identifying, prosecuting, and punishing witches. The treatise described witches as servants of Satan who used magick to harm Christians and advocated for brutal interrogation methods to force confessions.

This transformation in religious doctrine paved the way for the brutal witch-hunts in the early modern period. As the church's stance on witchcraft hardened, local superstitions became grounds for accusations of heresy and witchcraft. Widespread famine, disease, and social unrest exacerbated the situation, leading people to seek scapegoats for their suffering. The combination of deeply ingrained folk beliefs, church doctrine, and social tension created the conditions for mass persecution. By the 16th and 17th centuries, accusations of witchcraft had become a common way to express and resolve community fears. Having both religious and secular authorities actively promoting the hunt for witches. The persecution that followed would leave an enduring legacy. This not only shaped European society but influenced the American colonies as well, ultimately resulting in one of history's most infamous chapters: the witch-hunts.

CHAPTER 2

THE RISE OF WITCH-HUNTERS AND INQUISITORS

The driving forces behind witch-hunting in Europe were diverse and multifaceted, strengthening significantly over several centuries. This complexity reflects the intricate interplay of religious fervor, political control, and social fear. Each historical context, despite overlapping religious and secular motivations, uniquely influenced the persecution of suspected witches, dictating targets, methods, and punishment severity.

In the religious sphere, people often viewed the belief in witchcraft as a challenge to divine authority and a threat to the spiritual well-being of the community. The Church, in particular, played a significant role in promoting the belief in witches as agents of evil, justifying the persecution of those accused. Secular motivations were also at play, with political leaders using witch-hunts to merge power, suppress dissent, and maintain social order.

The distinct cultural, political, and social contexts of different regions in Europe shaped the manifestation of witch-hunting. For instance, in some areas, large-scale hunts and public trials characterized witch-hunting, while in others, it took the form of quieter, more insidious persecutions. The methods used and the severity of the punishments also varied, ranging from banishment and imprisonment to torture and execution.

In religious contexts, the hunt for witches was driven by theological convictions. Church authorities saw witchcraft as a mortal threat not only to individual souls but to the community's spiritual health. The association of witchcraft with Satan was paramount in medieval and early modern Europe. People considered witches heretics who had abandoned God and made deals with the Devil. This perception gained momentum as Christianity spread across Europe, condemning and seeking to replace pagan practices and folk magick. The Christian Church saw witches as embodiments of sin and disobedience, acting out Satan's will to subvert the divine order.

Key figures within the Church, such as Heinrich Kramer, co-author of the *Malleus Maleficarum* (1487), advocated for harsh measures against witches to protect Christian society from corruption. Kramer and other church officials believed that by hunting witches, they were combating Satan directly, purging society of his influence. This perspective found an institutional home with the establishment of the Inquisition, initially organized to address heresy in southern Europe and later expanded to include the prosecution of witches. Religious witch-hunts often viewed witches as an existential threat, leading to particularly severe punishments and elaborate trials designed to "save" the accused's soul while purging society of heretical contamination.

Secular motivations for witch-hunting were often pragmatic, tied to concerns over social order, control, and the enforcement of laws rather than spiritual salvation. Secular authorities saw witchcraft as a social and political threat, an illicit practice that destabilized communities. In regions where secular leaders held more authority, like some parts of Germany and England, secular authorities often pursued witch-hunts to reinforce law and order. They also used them to control marginalized populations, especially women, healers, and those outside of societal norms.

Witchcraft accusations also provided an easy way to target political or social rivals. Land disputes, local feuds, and power struggles often led to accusations of witchcraft to remove or discredit individuals. Secular courts in many areas treated witchcraft as a capital crime that warranted severe penalties, both to punish the accused and to deter others. Sometimes secular rulers saw witch trials as a way to demonstrate their power or protect their authority by quelling what they saw as morally corrupt or subversive practices.

Secular motivations often contributed to intense local outbreaks of witch-hunts, especially in regions where economic hardships, crop failures, or natural disasters caused social unrest. Fear and uncertainty frequently led communities to seek scapegoats, and accusations of witchcraft provided an outlet for these tensions. Unlike the religiously motivated Inquisition, secular authorities were less interested in the accused's repentance and more focused on their punishment and deterrence.

Several key figures, including witch-hunters, inquisitors, and self-proclaimed witch-finders, have significantly influenced witch-hunting through the ages. These individuals played a pivotal role in developing and enforcing the methods that defined the persecution of those accused of witchcraft. Their influence was profound, helping to shape societal perceptions of witchcraft and solidifying the harsh techniques used to identify, interrogate, and prosecute these individuals.

Witch-hunters, often motivated by a mix of fear, religious zealotry, and personal gain, helped to drive the witch-hunts. They implemented the often brutal methods used to investigate suspected witches. Inquisitors, typically associated with the Roman Catholic Church, were also significant figures in the history of witch-hunting. Inquisitors, whose job it was to eradicate heresy, often focused their efforts on those accused of witchcraft. Last, the so-called "witch-finders" were self-proclaimed experts in identifying witches, often traveling from town to town, spreading fear and accusations.

The combined efforts of these figures created a climate of fear and suspicion, leading to the widespread persecution of those accused of witchcraft. Their actions helped to solidify the methods used in the identification, interrogation, and prosecution of suspected witches, shaping the course of witch-hunting history.

The Inquisition, established by the Catholic Church in the 13th century, was initially focused on rooting out heresy but eventually expanded to include witchcraft. Early inquisitors like Bernard Gui and Nicholas Eymerich set the precedent for rigorous investigations, using coercive methods to extract confessions. Eymerich's *Directorium Inquisitorum* outlined techniques for interrogating heretics, many of which would later apply to accused witches. This text provided guidance on torture, forced confessions, and interpreting evidence, and it endorsed the use of extreme measures to get confessions when dealing with supposed threats to the Church.

Dominican inquisitors Heinrich Kramer and Jacob Sprenger cemented the Inquisition's focus on witchcraft with the publication of the *Malleus Maleficarum* in 1487. This text outlined various methods for identifying and interrogating witches and framed witchcraft as a Satanic conspiracy, requiring extreme vigilance and punishment. The *Malleus* contributed significantly to the rise of witch trials across Europe, laying out a framework that demonized witches and justified the use of torture to extract confessions. Kramer, especially, fueled fear, claiming witches were everywhere and only relentless persecution could destroy them.

Beyond the institutional authority of the Inquisition, independent witch-hunters emerged who operated outside the church's authority. Many of them often worked in tandem with or for secular rulers. One of the most infamous witch-finders was Matthew Hopkins, the self-styled "Witchfinder General" of England, active in the 1640s. Hopkins exploited social fear and local grievances to fuel a witch-hunt frenzy, leading to the execution of over a hundred people. His methods included the infamous "swimming test," where accused witches were bound and thrown into the water. Authorities declared those who floated guilty because they believed water would reject "unholy" bodies. If they sank and drowned, they were innocent. Hopkins and his associate, John Stearne, operated for profit, charging communities fees for each witch they identified. This commercial aspect of witch-hunting amplified public fear and created a lucrative incentive for identifying witches, leading to a rapid escalation in accusations.

In France, inquisitors like Pierre de Lancre took on a more authoritarian role, using witch-hunts to reassert Catholic control over regions that resisted church authority. De Lancre's zeal for rooting out "heretical" practices was so intense that he was responsible for the deaths of hundreds in the Basque region. This is where he believed the witches congregated in covens. His methods included extensive use of torture to coerce confessions. He often forced suspects to implicate others, spreading the web of suspicion and fear.

Many early witch-hunters developed or adapted methods of interrogation that relied on torture, driven by the belief that witches would not confess without duress. In Scotland and parts of England, the practice of "witch pricking" became a common method of identifying witches. Witch-prickers would use needles or specially designed tools to prick the accused's skin. This supposedly allowed them to look for spots that didn't bleed or were "insensitive" to pain, believed to be marks of a pact with the Devil. In some places, authorities used scratching, a method where supposed victims scratched the accused to draw blood, believing this would weaken the witch's power over them.

Particularly in the inquisitorial courts, inquisitors commonly used the rack, the strappado (where they hung victims by their wrists and dropped them suddenly), and other torture devices to extract confessions. Such devices inflicted extreme physical pain, often leading the accused to confess simply to end their suffering. These brutal tactics were justified by the belief that witches, as servants of Satan, would lie unless coerced.

Another tactic used by both church and secular authorities was sleep deprivation, keeping suspects awake for days as a form of psychological torture. They believed this method weakened the accused's resistance, making them more likely to confess under pressure.

The influence of early witch-hunters, inquisitors, and witch-finders like Kramer, Hopkins, and de Lancre had a profound and lasting impact. They created a framework where witches were not merely criminals but existential threats to both the church and society, justifying the use of extreme measures. They relied on coercion, torture, and fearmongering in their methods. This set a precedent that spread across Europe and eventually to the American colonies, fueling widespread witch trials that devastated communities. This era led to the deaths of forty to sixty thousand innocent people.

By establishing legal and theological justifications for the witch-hunts, these historic figures embedded a culture of fear that influenced society at all levels. The hysteria drew ordinary people in, leading them to accuse their neighbors and even family members of witchcraft. Inquisitors, witch-finders, and secular officials built a powerful mechanism of control, turning community tensions, personal vendettas, and religious zeal into deadly accusations.

CHAPTER 3
THE TESTS AND TORTURES OF WITCH TRIALS

Test Methods

Distressing methods were used to detect and punish individuals suspected of practicing witchcraft, which characterizes the historical landscape of these types of accusations. Witch trials employed a variety of "tests" based on superstitions and widely accepted, yet frequently irrational, beliefs about the abilities and conduct of witches. These tests, when showing that an individual might be a witch, often led to the use of torture to coerce confessions. The methods of torture were diverse and severe, ranging from the brutal crushing of limbs to the cruel practice of sleep deprivation. These approaches, both the so-called tests and the torturous punishments, underscore the extreme and frequently lethal measures societies would take in their fear driven endeavors to eradicate witchcraft. This discourse delves into some of the most infamous methods used to "test" for witchcraft and torment the accused, revealing the harsh and unjust nature of these historical practices.

During the 16th and 17th centuries, witch-pricking emerged as a popular method for identifying supposed witches. This procedure was based on the belief that witches bore a "witch's-mark," a spot on the body that was insensitive to pain or would not bleed when pierced. Folklore and religious superstition rooted the idea, suggesting that the devil placed this mark on his followers as a seal of allegiance. This belief led to the employment of professional witch-prickers. Tasking these individuals with the grisly job of locating these marks on accused persons' bodies. This mark is different than the apotropaic marks which are referred to as witch's marks. This type of mark was craved near doors, windows and even caves as a protection symbol.

Witch-prickers, such as the infamous Christian Caddell, who called herself John Dickson, would carry out their examinations using sharp needles, knives, or custom-made pricking instruments. They would systematically pierce the skin of the accused in search of the "witch's-mark." Restraining the person being pricked, the procedure could last hours, as prickers would scrutinize every inch of skin. Upon finding a spot that did not produce pain or bleeding, prickers considered it conclusive evidence of witchcraft. This test, however, was highly subjective and open to manipulation. They often interpreted innocuous skin blemishes such as birthmarks, scars, or even moles as "witch-marks," that effectively condemned innocent people.

The procedure's accuracy was notoriously dubious. Many times, witch-prickers used retractable blades, designed to create the illusion of a "mark" by pricking without causing pain or visible injury. This deception allowed witch-prickers to "prove" a lack of response, solidifying accusations without actual evidence. Witch-prickers labeled countless innocent people as witches, based on fabricated or exaggerated findings. People rarely questioned the witch-pricker's fraudulent techniques because fear and superstition about witchcraft were so widespread that few dared to challenge these practices.

Many of these witch-prickers received payment for each witch they identified, making their role often financially motivated. This created a troubling conflict of interest, as the more "witches" they uncovered, the greater their earnings. Given the environment of suspicion and fear, prickers like Caddell wielded significant influence, their accusations leading to imprisonment, torture, and, frequently, execution. This period saw untold numbers of individuals falsely accused and punished, based solely on the pseudoscientific methods employed by these so-called experts.

The "swimming test," also known as "dunking" or "floating," was one of the most infamous and perilous methods employed during the witch trials, particularly in Europe and colonial America. The belief that witches, as agents of the devil, would reject baptismal water, symbolizing purity and sanctity, fueled the use of the "swimming test." This superstition led to the assumption that water, a symbol of spiritual purity, would refuse to accept those who had renounced Christianity and allied themselves with evil forces. If an accused witch floated, authorities would interpret it as "proof" that the water had rejected them, confirming their guilt. Conversely, if the accused sank, the water accepted them, which meant they were innocent.

To carry out the test, the accused person's hands and feet were tightly bound, often leaving them with little to no mobility. They then tossed or dropped the accused person into a body of water, typically a pond or river. Observers would watch to see whether the accused floated or sank. The logic behind this test was paradoxical and cruel; floating resulted in a guilty verdict, often leading to execution, while sinking showed innocence but presented its own fatal risk. Those who sank had to rely on the vigilance of bystanders to pull them out in time to avoid drowning. However, many times, delays or outright neglect meant that innocent individuals tragically lost their lives.

The test's deadly implications underscore the extent of fear and irrationality that permeated the witch-hunting mindset. The swimming test was not only a life-threatening ordeal but also an example of a test in which the accused could not win. Either outcome could lead to harm or death. Even when someone was "proven" innocent by sinking, the near-death experience left lasting trauma. Accusations often still followed them, as townsfolk were hesitant to abandon suspicion.

Despite its dangers and the high risk of wrongful death, the swimming test gained popularity because of its simplicity and visual drama. It didn't require specialized equipment or knowledge and was easy for anyone to administer in local rivers or ponds. The public nature of the test also served as a spectacle, reinforcing fear of witchcraft among the community while promoting unity against perceived threats. Sometimes, this ritualized punishment, although rooted in cruelty and prejudice, fostered social bonding through the community's collective participation.

The "Prayer Test" was a widely used method in witch trials, particularly during the height of witch hysteria in early modern Europe and colonial America. This was based on the belief that witches, as followers of the devil, could not properly recite sacred Christian texts. This test required the accused to recite specific items flawlessly, like the *Lord's Prayer*. They believed that because witches had renounced their faith, they lost their connection to the divine, which made them incapable of reciting God's words properly. Those who tested witches viewed any stumble, mispronunciation, or pause in the recitation as a failure of the test, which they considered a sign of guilt.

This was a subtle but potent tool in a witch trial, as it relied heavily on the psychological state of the accused. The test design offered little mercy. Suspects were often nervous, terrified, and under enormous pressure, which made mistakes all but inevitable. The fear of facing accusations of witchcraft, a crime punishable by torture or even death, would understandably lead to anxiety. This could cause even devout individuals to falter or forget words. Accusers often interpreted these natural human reactions as signs of malevolence or guilt. The test administrators showed little regard for the high-pressure circumstances.

This test was further complicated by language barriers and literacy levels. In many rural or less educated communities, people might not have known the *Lord's Prayer* by heart, particularly if they were not fluent in Latin. People traditionally learned the prayer in Latin during that period. Those who struggled with the language or who were not regular churchgoers were especially vulnerable. This was true for older individuals, the uneducated, or those with cognitive or speech impairments. In these cases, the Prayer Test became more a reflection of social biases than an actual test of piety or allegiance to the church.

The inherent flaws of the Prayer Test lay in its subjective nature and its disregard for the impact of fear on memory and speech. Authorities administering the test often sought to find guilt, driven by prevailing superstitions and community pressures to rid society of perceived threats. If an accused person stumbled over the words or showed any hesitation, those administering the test assumed the devil was interfering with their speech. Conversely, even if an accused person recited the prayer perfectly, accusers might still claim the devil empowered them to feign piety. This is a classic example of "damned if you do and damned if you don't."

Despite its lack of objectivity, authorities widely considered the Prayer Test a straightforward and definitive method for identifying witchcraft among ordinary townsfolk. This approach had the advantage of being easily accessible, as it required no special tools or extensive preparation. The simplicity of the test made it an appealing choice for communities who were eager to uncover supposed witches, particularly in times of heightened anxiety and fear.

However, this same simplicity also concealed the test's cruel and inefficient design. By setting an impossible standard under such stressful conditions, the Prayer Test essentially ensured that the outcome would confirm the guilt of the accused. The test required individuals to recite prayers with no hesitation, stumbling, or error, which was an incredibly challenging task even for those not under suspicion of witchcraft. The stress and pressure of the situation often led to mistakes, which were then interpreted as signs of guilt.

This method, while seemingly less invasive than other tests, was not without its flaws. The Prayer Test relied heavily on the subjective interpretations of the observers, who may have been influenced by their own fears and prejudices. The test placed a significant burden on the accused, requiring them to remain calm, composed, and flawless under intense scrutiny and duress.

The Prayer Test was a method that, while easy to administer, was deeply flawed and open to manipulation. Its design ensured that the accused would likely fail, reinforcing the community's fears and prejudices. This test, like many others used during the witch trials, highlights the dangers of unchecked superstition and the failure of reasoned justice.

The "Touch Test" was a widely employed method in medieval Europe, particularly during the height of the witch-hunts, to determine whether an individual was indeed a witch. Where an alleged victim claimed to be afflicted by a witch's curse or spirit, witch-hunters often used this test. The supposed victim was typically a family member, neighbor, or someone with a grudge against the accused. The procedure involved the accused being asked to touch the afflicted individual, usually a child or a vulnerable adult, to break the alleged curse or spirit's hold.

If the victim's symptoms, such as convulsions, fits, or other physical manifestations of distress, ceased upon contact with the accused, witch-hunters considered it conclusive proof of the accused's guilt. This was based on the misguided belief that a witch's physical touch had the power to break their own spell or curse. However, the test was deeply flawed and often led to tragic consequences for the accused. Psychological relief or fear often caused symptoms to cease, but witch-hunters misinterpreted this as a sign of guilt, further solidifying the accused's fate.

The Touch Test exemplified the era's profound misunderstandings of physical and mental health. People did not yet understand the concept of psychological relief and the power of suggestion. As a result, they often interpreted the accused's actions as a sign of guilt rather than a natural response to the stress and fear of being accused.

"Spectral Evidence" is testimony that relied on the accusers' claims of encountering the "specter" or spirit of the accused. This became a notorious aspect of the Salem Witch Trials of 1692. This type of evidence was based on the accusers' assertions that they had seen or experienced visions or dreams where the accused appeared. Most often, with the accused intending to cause harm or exerting control over them. Both the witch-hunters and townsfolk accepted the testimonies describing these apparitions as conclusive proof of witchcraft, even though only the accuser could claim to have seen or experienced these specters. This reliance on spectral evidence was problematic, as it was impossible to verify or disprove, leaving it to the subjective accounts of the accusers.

Using spectral evidence was a hallmark of the Salem Witch Trials, where the atmosphere of fear and hysteria was palpable. Accusers, often young girls and women, would claim to have seen the accused's specter in their dreams or visions, describing vivid details of the apparition's appearance and actions. These testimonies were often used to corroborate other evidence, such as physical symptoms or behavioral changes, and were frequently used to incriminate the accused. However, the use of spectral evidence was deeply flawed. It was based on the accusers' personal experiences and perceptions, which were often influenced by their own fears, biases, and superstitions.

The reliance on spectral evidence revealed the deeply irrational and fearful mindset of the time, as well as the inherent flaws in trials based solely on personal accusations and dreams. Using this type of evidence showed a lack of understanding of the human psyche. It was also an example of the power of suggestion, as well as a willingness to accept unsubstantiated claims as proof of guilt.

The "Weighing Test" was another dubious method employed in the witch trials, reflecting a widespread superstition that witches possessed an unnatural lightness. In some regions, authorities would weigh the accused against a stack of Bibles or a set standard of weight. This was under the assumption that a genuine witch would weigh less than expected. This idea stemmed from the belief that witches could defy natural laws and manipulate their physical bodies to achieve an unnatural state of levity. However, this test was not only arbitrary but also fundamentally flawed. Science has taught us weight can vary because of a multitude of normal biological factors, such as age, sex, body composition, and hydration levels.

However, this approach was inherently inaccurate and prone to misinterpretation. This approach mislabeled lighter individuals as witches, regardless of their innocence. The approach could also wrongly declare a heavier individual innocent. The Weighing Test was also susceptible to manipulation, as authorities could easily manipulate the results by adjusting the number of Bibles or weights used in the test. A basic lack of scientific rigor and reliance on superstition resulted in the execution of many innocent people. Authorities wrongly accused and condemned them based on the flawed and arbitrary Weighing Test.

The Weighing Test, like other methods employed in the witch trials, showcased the absence of genuine evidence and the extent to which superstition shaped justice during this period. Using such methods highlights the dangers of allowing fear, ignorance, and superstition to guide the administration of justice, often at the expense of innocent lives. These tests remain a stark reminder of the importance of upholding the principles of due process and evidence-based decision-making. A reminder of protecting human rights, particularly in the face of overwhelming public hysteria and fear.

Methods of Torture

In the early modern period, many religious and legal authorities believed witches were agents of the Devil, posing a moral and physical threat to society. Consequently, torturing accused witches to get confessions was not only acceptable but deemed a moral obligation. The medieval church, influenced by figures like Pope Innocent VIII (with his bull *Summis desiderantes* in 1484), authorized the use of torture to combat heresy and witchcraft. Later, the publication of the *Malleus Maleficarum* (1487) by Heinrich Kramer and Jacob Sprenger further justified and codified torture methods. They argue witches would only confess under intense duress because of their "hardened" allegiance to Satan.

Authorities believed that torture would "purge" the accused of heresy, leading them to renounce Satan and embrace repentance. Legal codes like the *Constitutio Criminalis Carolina* (1532), Germany's criminal code, laid out detailed guidelines for torturing accused witches, reflecting a broader societal acceptance of these extreme measures.

The tortures used during the Inquisition and the witch trials reveal a time when fear and superstition overruled human compassion. This lack of compassion drove authorities to commit unspeakable acts against men, women, and children. These tortures broke both body and spirit, often leaving the accused with lifelong physical and psychological wounds, if they survived at all. While meant to eliminate heresy and witchcraft, these methods ultimately revealed the horrifying cruelty of the era.

One of the most commonly used torture devices was the "strappado", also known as "reverse hanging." In this method, the accused's hands were bound behind their back with a rope tied to their wrists. Then they would hoist them into the air. After suspending the accused, executioners often added weights to their feet, causing excruciating pain in the shoulders and joints, sometimes leading to dislocation.

The strappado was effective in obtaining confessions, as the pain was so intense that it frequently led to compliance. However, this method often left lasting injuries, both physical and psychological. Inquisitors and witch-hunters across Europe, especially in Italy and France, widely used the strappado. Records of its use exist in witch trials throughout the continent.

The "thumbscrew" was a smaller, more targeted instrument of torture, but no less painful. This device comprised a metal clamp that was placed over the thumb, fingers, or toes, and then tightened by turning a screw. The pressure crushed the bones of the digits, causing excruciating pain and often permanent disfigurement.

While not as dramatic as other forms of torture, the thumbscrew was effective in causing intense, localized pain. Its portability made it a popular choice for inquisitors who wanted to inflict pain quickly without setting up larger, more elaborate devices. German and Swiss inquisitors and witch-hunters widely used thumbscrews during the witch trials. Many of the accused witches confessed under the agonizing pain inflicted by this small device.

The "rack" was one of the most notorious torture devices of the medieval and early modern period. Its design stretched the body to unnatural lengths. The accused was bound at the wrists and ankles and placed on a rectangular frame. Executioners and witch-hunters would turn rollers on each end of the rack, gradually pulling the limbs in opposite directions to stretch muscles, ligaments, and joints.

The pain caused by the rack was so intense that it often led to immediate confessions. English, French, and Spanish witch trials frequently employed the rack. Often, its mere presence compelled the accused to cooperate. The rack inflicted long-term physical damage, and many times, permanently disabled its victims, if they survived.

The "Scavenger's Daughter" was a metal device shaped like a triangle that compressed the body rather than stretching it. They placed the accused in a crouched position and bound their head, knees, and wrists tightly together. This device then squeezed the body inward, leading to intense cramping, difficulty breathing, and excruciating pain.

Although less common than the rack, authorities used the Scavenger's Daughter in both England and Spain. Its compact design made it easy to transport, and its effect on the body was equally damaging, often leaving the accused unable to stand or walk afterward.

The boot, or "Spanish Boot", was a device that comprised a series of iron or wooden splints that were tightened around the leg, crushing the bones and soft tissues. It was a popular device in Scotland and France. After securing the boot, someone would then drive wedges between the leg and splints, generating enormous pressure that fractured the bones.

Used for both preliminary and final torture, the sight of the boot alone was usually enough to intimidate the accused into confessing. This torture frequently resulted in shattered bones and permanent disfigurement for those who lived through it.

The "Witch's Bridle", also known as the "Scold's Bridle", was a medieval torture device used to punish women accused of being gossips, naggers, or witches. This gruesome device comprised an iron muzzle with a framework that enclosed the head, a bit or curb-plate that slid into the mouth. There was a chain or leash attached to the side to lead or chain the accused to something. Spikes or sharp edges often adorned the iron muzzle, adding to the wearer's discomfort and humiliation.

The Witch's Bridle silenced the wearer, preventing them from speaking or shouting. The bit or curb-plate, often spiked, pressed down on the tongue, causing discomfort and silencing the wearer. This punishment would humiliate and shame the accused, often leading them through town or displaying them on a town cross. The iron muzzle and chain or leash also made the wearer appear ridiculous, serving as a public spectacle.

Historical records mention the use of the Witch's Bridle as a punishment for women accused of not just witchcraft, but gossiping, or nagging as well. For example, in 1590, King James I examined Agnes Sampson and fastened her to her cell wall with a witch's bridle, an iron instrument with four sharp prongs. With this device, King James I's investigators extracted a confession from Sampson, who faced accusations of witchcraft and ultimately executed.

Using the Witch's Bridle was not limited to England, Scotland, and Wales. Other parts of Europe, including Germany and France, also used similar devices. Witch-hunters often used the device with other forms of punishment, such as public flogging or imprisonment. The Witch's Bridle served as a tool of oppression, silencing and shaming women accused of being witches.

Townsfolk would often burn or brand those already convicted as a means of "purifying" the accused of witchcraft. A common method involved placing a hot iron on the skin, usually on the arms or torso, causing severe burns. Sometimes, they branded the accused with a symbol, such as a cross, to mark their perceived guilt or to "cleanse" them of the Devil's influence.

This method was common in many parts of Europe, including Germany and France, and authorities sometimes used it to degrade victims before execution. Branding left permanent scars, both physical and psychological, serving as a lasting reminder of the witch-hunting hysteria.

Besides physical torture, authorities used psychological tactics to break down the accused. A common tactic involved prolonged isolation, where they would keep the accused alone for days or weeks, limiting their food and contact with others. This isolation caused extreme mental anguish and heightened the accused's sense of helplessness, making them more likely to confess.

Sleep deprivation was another widely used tactic. Guards or interrogators would question them relentlessly, keeping the accused awake for days. This exhaustion weakened their mental defenses, leading to confusion and often prompting confessions. The psychological impact of these tactics, combined with physical torture, created a terrifying environment from which many believed the only escape was confession.

Using torture in the witch trials had catastrophic effects on the accused. Many confessed under duress, admitting to acts of witchcraft they had not committed simply to end their suffering. The confessions were often inconsistent, exaggerated, and riddled with fantastical elements, yet authorities accepted them as genuine, being desperate to prove the existence of witches.

Torture inflicted both physical and psychological trauma on survivors, leaving lasting scars. Although some of these survivors, being cleared of any wrongdoing, never fully recovered from the trauma inflicted by torture. Families of the accused were also deeply affected, bearing the social stigma of being associated with a "witch" and often losing their livelihoods because of the reputational damage.

The methods of torture used in the witch-hunts have left an indelible mark on history. It illustrates the lengths to which society will go to root out perceived threats. These techniques, sanctioned by both church and state, reflect a period where fear, superstition, and a fervent desire for control fueled unimaginable cruelty. The legacy of this brutality lives on as a reminder of the dangers of mass hysteria and the abuse of authority.

CHAPTER 4
KRAMER, SPRENGER, AND THE MALLEUS MALEFICARUM

Heinrich Kramer and Jacob Sprenger, two Dominican inquisitors, are most famously known as the authors of the *Malleus Maleficarum*, a treatise on witchcraft that was published in 1487. This text, whose title translates to the "*Hammer of Witches*," became one of the most notorious and influential manuals on witch-hunting in European history. The book's impact was profound, shaping the way people perceived and dealt with accusations of witchcraft for centuries to come.

They are both credited as co-authors, although scholars continue to debate Sprenger's actual contribution. Some evidence suggests that Kramer may have been the primary author and only added Sprenger's name to lend credibility to the work. This seems plausible given Sprenger's high-ranking position as a Dominican inquisitor in the Holy Roman Empire. Regardless of authorship disputes, the book combined their authority and Dominican positions, giving the *Malleus* legitimacy in the eyes of both religious and secular authorities. This legitimacy was crucial, as the book's influence extended far beyond the confines of the Catholic Church, shaping the witch-hunts that swept across Europe during the 16th and 17th centuries.

Kramer's personal obsession with witchcraft and his zealous religious fervor set the stage for the book's creation. Known for his rigid orthodoxy and intolerance toward what he considered heretical or sinful practices, Kramer held deeply misogynistic views, believing women to be susceptible to temptation and evil influence. An unsuccessful witch trial he had conducted in Innsbruck in 1485, where local clergy denounced his methods, partially fueled his views, calling them improper and exaggerated. Undeterred by this setback, Kramer returned to Germany and began compiling the *Malleus Maleficarum*, aiming to create an authoritative guide for rooting out witchcraft.

Sprenger, a fellow Dominican with a prestigious academic reputation, lent the project additional weight. A professor of theology and a respected figure within the Church, he was a counterbalance to Kramer's extreme zealotry. Together, their work was a systematic and unyielding tool to eradicate witches, addressing theological, practical, and legal concerns surrounding witchcraft. The *Malleus Maleficarum* aimed to guide inquisitors in identifying, trying, and punishing witches, spreading the belief that witches posed a real and pressing threat to the Christian world.

The *Malleus Maleficarum* presented a detailed, and disturbing, blueprint for identifying and prosecuting accused witches. It provided a comprehensive guide for those tasked with rooting out and punishing those deemed guilty of witchcraft. The book comprises three separate sections, each focusing on a different aspect of witchcraft and persecution. The first section delves into the theological justifications for the existence of witches. It draws on biblical passages and Church doctrine to establish the notion that witchcraft is a real and present threat to society. This section sets the stage for the rest of the book. The text argues that society must identify and punish witches, not as misguided people, but as tools of the Devil.

In this part, Kramer and Sprenger sought to establish that witches, especially female witches, were a genuine threat and had made pacts with the Devil. They argued that denying the existence of witchcraft was itself a heresy, aligning disbelief with a rejection of Church teachings. The *Malleus* explicitly claims that women are particularly susceptible to witchcraft because of their "weakness" in character and intellect. They based this view on biblical references and a highly patriarchal interpretation of Christian doctrine. This misogynistic perspective is a core tenet of the *Malleus*, which repeatedly asserts that women's supposed susceptibility to sin makes them the ideal instruments of Satan.

The authors referenced Eve's fall from grace as a sign of inherent feminine weakness and vulnerability to temptation. They claimed women were more likely to be "seduced" by the Devil. Kramer and Sprenger also attributed witchcraft to women's sexuality, claiming that women used their charms to manipulate and deceive men. This focus on a woman's supposed moral failings and tendency toward deception only reinforced gender biases of the time. It also laid the groundwork for a misogynistic approach to witch-hunting. Women became primary targets in the witch-hunts that followed, as the *Malleus* associated witchcraft with femininity and promiscuity, casting accusations on women whose behavior deviated from perceived social norms.

The second section focuses on methods for identifying witches, including descriptions of their supposed physical characteristics, behaviors, and habits. It also provides guidance on how to interrogate accused witches, including the use of torture to extract confessions.

The *Malleus* provided specific methods for identifying witches. Kramer and Sprenger suggested inquisitors look for signs of a witch's pact with the Devil, including physical marks (known as witch-marks), odd behavior, or involvement in folk practices or herbalism. Suspicious behavior could include anything from muttering strange words to displaying unusual knowledge or independence. Widows, healers, midwives, and those who lived alone were particularly vulnerable to accusation.

Kramer and Sprenger advocated for harsh interrogative practices to "unmask" the accused, even endorsing torture as a legitimate means of obtaining confessions. They believed witches would not admit to their crimes without coercion, as Satan was supposedly protecting them. The authors argued that extreme measures, such as sleep deprivation and physical torture, were necessary tools for obtaining the truth. They claimed divine intervention would eventually free innocent individuals if wrongfully accused. The *Malleus* legitimized the use of torture in the witch trials, contributing to widespread and often brutal practices that resulted in many accused falsely confessing to end their suffering.

The third and final section offers guidance on prosecuting those found guilty, including advice on how to conduct trials, gather evidence, and impose sentences. Throughout the book, Kramer and Sprenger (or Kramer alone, depending on the authorship debate) demonstrate a clear bias against accused witches. They viewed them as a threat to the established social order and the Church's authority.

In this last section, the *Malleus* outlined the judicial process for trying accused witches, emphasizing the importance of swift and decisive action to prevent the spread of witchcraft. Kramer and Sprenger offered practical advice on handling witnesses and evidence, advising that even hearsay or uncorroborated accusations could be sufficient for conviction if the accused exhibited signs of witchcraft. The authors encouraged inquisitors to discount any defenses the accused might offer, as they believed witches would lie or use magick to manipulate the court.

The *Malleus* dismissed the need for evidence that would meet the rigorous standards of secular law. Asserting that the nature of witchcraft required a unique and lenient approach to gather evidence. For instance, the *Malleus* suggested courts admit "spectral evidence," which is testimony that someone saw the apparition of the accused committing witchcraft. Using this type of standards for evidence created a system in which the accused were nearly always found guilty, with the *Malleus* explicitly cautioning judges against showing mercy. They argued it would only embolden witches and endanger Christian society.

The *Malleus Maleficarum* had a profound and far-reaching impact on the witch-hunts that would engulf Europe over the next two centuries. This lone text left a trail of devastation and death in its wake. While some Church authorities initially condemned the *Malleus Maleficarum* for its extreme views and methods, the text's persuasive tone and the authority of its authors ultimately prevailed. This made it a widely accepted and influential guide for those seeking to combat the perceived threat of witches. As fear of witchcraft grew in the 16th and 17th centuries, the *Malleus* became a staple text for inquisitors, judges, and magistrates across Europe. They referenced it as a trusted source of guidance on how to identify, prosecute, and punish those accused of witchcraft.

The manual influenced more than the Catholic regions. With the Protestant Reformation and the Counter-Reformation fueling religious tensions, the *Malleus* found an audience among both Catholic and Protestant authorities. As Protestant regions broke away from the Catholic Church, they maintained and even intensified witch-hunting practices. Seeing them as a means to purify their communities and rid themselves of perceived threats to their new faiths. The manual's influence helped standardize and amplify the witch-hunting methods across Germany, France, Switzerland, and the British Isles, contributing to the execution of thousands of people accused of witchcraft. The *Malleus Maleficarum's* impact went beyond the number of lives lost. This text also helped to create a culture of fear and suspicion, where accusations of witchcraft became a tool for social control and personal gain.

The *Malleus Maleficarum's* most damaging legacy is perhaps its role in normalizing torture and unreliable evidence in witch trials. This set a disturbing precedent that would have far-reaching consequences for centuries to come. The book justified extreme methods as necessary measures in a holy war against Satanic forces. Thus, many authorities adopted its guidelines without question, often disregarding the principles of due process and protecting human rights. The *Malleus's* influence led to a legal culture that accepted confessions, obtained by using torture and other forms of coercion, as reliable evidence. Authorities also widely accepted the use of "spectral" evidence, such as testimony from witnesses who claimed to have seen apparitions or heard voices.

This created a toxic environment where mass hysteria and false accusations could thrive, turning communities against their own members and leading to the execution of countless innocent people. The *Malleus's* focus on women as primary suspects led to widespread persecution of women, particularly those who lived outside traditional social roles, such as midwives, healers, widows, and outspoken women. Accusations and executions disproportionately targeted these already marginalized and vulnerable women, creating a culture of fear that stifled women's autonomy and reinforced gender hierarchies. By targeting these groups, the *Malleus* contributed to a legacy of gendered violence, casting women as agents of the Devil. This subjected them to horrific fates, including torture, imprisonment, and execution. The book's influence also perpetuated the notion that women were inherently more susceptible to demonic influence, and that their roles in society were inherently suspect. This culture of suspicion and mistrust viewed women as potential threats to the social order, and often deemed their lives expendable.

Unfortunately, the *Malleus Maleficarum* remained influential well into the 17th century. It guided inquisitors during some of the most infamous witch-hunts, including the Würzburg and Bamberg trials in Germany and the Pendle Witch Trials in England. Even after its decline as a primary reference, its themes persisted in European legal systems. These systems continued to treat accusations of witchcraft as a criminal offense well into the 18th century. The *Malleus Maleficarum's* impact endured far beyond its time. Having influence not only the legal proceedings of its day but also leaving a dark imprint on history as one of the deadliest tools of medieval and early modern persecution.

CHAPTER 5
MATTHEW HOPKINS IS THE WITCHFINDER GENERAL

The story of Matthew Hopkins, known as the Witchfinder General, is one of infamy, fear, and exploitation. He operated in England during a period of intense social, political, and religious upheaval. His methods were brutal and ruthless, leading to the persecution and death of many individuals, mostly women, accused of witchcraft. Hopkins became the most notorious witch-hunter of the English Civil War era. The English Civil Wars comprised three wars, which were fought between Charles I and Parliament between 1642 and 1651. These wars were part of a wider conflict involving Wales, Scotland and Ireland, known as the Wars of the Three Kingdoms.

Matthew Hopkins' career as a witch-hunter began in the 1640s, a decade marked by profound upheaval and transformation in England. The English Civil War engulfed the nation. This period of civil strife led to widespread social dislocation, economic hardship, and a deepening of religious tensions. As communities grappled with the surrounding chaos, they increasingly turned to supernatural explanations for the misfortunes and instability they faced. Amidst this backdrop of paranoia, Hopkins emerged, exploiting these fears and establishing himself as the self-appointed "Witchfinder General."

With little known about his early life, historians believe that Matthew Hopkins was born in Wenham, Suffolk, around 1620. He was the son of a Puritan minister, and the strict and straight forward values of the Puritan faith deeply influenced his upbringing. This upbringing instilled in him a strong sense of moral rectitude and a deep-seated hostility toward what he perceived as ungodly behavior. This would later become a hallmark of his approach to witch-hunting.

The young Matthew Hopkins was reportedly well-educated and came from a relatively prosperous family, which would have provided him with a solid foundation for his future endeavors. However, despite his privileged background, Hopkins lacked formal training as a lawyer or magistrate. Given his later career choice, it seems likely that he would have had formal legal training. Instead, he displayed an unusual ambition and a talent for manipulation. A talent that would significantly affect his rise to prominence as a witch-hunter.

Hopkins' career as a witch-hunter began in earnest around 1644, and his rise was sudden and meteoric. Initially, communities recognized Hopkins as an expert in identifying witches, and his claims of expertise went unchallenged, at least in the beginning. He styled himself the "Witchfinder General," a title that suggested an authority and level of expertise that was self-proclaimed. His methods and claims went unchallenged, allowing him to move from town to town, conducting "investigations" and overseeing brutal interrogations. He often used techniques that were just a little short of torture to extract confessions from his victims.

Historians have debated Hopkins' motivations, considering factors like religious fervor, personal ambition, and financial gain. While his Puritan background certainly fueled a genuine hatred of what he considered ungodly practices, Hopkins also charged towns and villages for his services, earning substantial fees. Some argue that greed motivated his actions as much as religious conviction, given that his witch-hunting activities brought him both profit and notoriety. Hopkins capitalized on the religious and political instability of the time, casting himself as a figure of authority against perceived forces of evil.

The towns and villages knew of Hopkins for his exceptionally ruthless methods. Unlike other parts of Europe, where church courts primarily oversaw witch-hunting, Hopkins worked within the unique context of English common law, which typically discouraged torture. However, he circumvented these restrictions, employing methods that were technically outside the formal definition of torture but were still agonizing and effective in coercing confessions.

One of Hopkins' primary methods was "witch-pricking," a practice involving the examination of the accused for "witch-marks." Witch-marks were physical signs of a pact with the Devil. These marks, according to Hopkins, could be small moles, scars, or blemishes that did not bleed or cause pain when pricked. They would strip the accused completely naked in front of the court and then shave them from head to toe. Hopkins or his assistants would use a specially crafted needle to poke these spots. Often, the needles used were retractable or blunted to avoid causing bleeding or pain, creating the illusion that the accused had an unnatural "Devil's mark." This was really nothing more than a form of horrendous sexual abuse. In a society that held modesty in high regard, many women would confess just to end their humiliation.

Witch-pricking was extremely manipulative, as it preyed on the accused's ignorance and fear. The witch-pricker could interpret any unusual physical feature as evidence of a pact with Satan. This effectively made the test meaningless from an evidentiary standpoint. It remained as a powerful psychological tool, giving Hopkins and his assistants a façade of scientific rigor and infallibility.

Hopkins also relied on the notorious "swimming test," a harrowing ordeal because people believed water would reject witches. In this test, the accused would be bound and lowered into a body of water. People believed that if the accused floated, they were guilty, but if they sank, they were innocent. Authorities reasoned that, because witches had renounced their baptism, the water would reject them, a notion based on flawed religious logic.

The theory behind the swimming test was itself life-threatening. The accused, bound with ropes, risked drowning if they sank. Hopkins and his assistants completely controlled the outcome, making it nearly impossible for the accused to escape suspicion. This test became emblematic of Hopkins' cruel and relentless approach, demonstrating his willingness to subject people to dangerous and humiliating ordeals to extract confessions.

Hopkins also frequently used sleep deprivation as a method to weaken the accused and induce confessions. His assistants would keep the accused awake for extended periods, sometimes days, believing that sleeplessness would make them more susceptible to admitting guilt. This practice, though not very violent, was psychologically grueling and highly effective in breaking the resistance of even the most resolute individuals. The accused would often confess simply to end the ordeal, further solidifying Hopkins' reputation as a successful witch-finder.

This combination of pricking, swimming tests, and sleep deprivation created a harrowing experience for the accused. The trials often left the accused isolated, physically exhausted, and terrified. These methods reinforced the widespread belief in witchcraft, as each confession received through torture and coercion seemed to confirm witches were living within the community.

The Chelmsford trials were one of Matthew Hopkins' most notorious episodes. These trials took place in Essex, a region in eastern England. This is where he claimed to have uncovered a nest of witches. In March 1645, Hopkins and his associate, John Stearne, arrived in the town, stirring up fear and suspicion among the local population. Hopkins and Stearne, presenting themselves as witchcraft authorities. After arriving in the town, they generated a mixture of fascination and terror among the townsfolk. Accusations of witchcraft proliferated rapidly, often targeting women who were either socially marginalized or known for unconventional behavior, such as midwives, healers, and widows.

Hopkins applied his methods rigorously and used a range of techniques to extract confessions from the accused. These included the "pricking method," where he would examine the accused for signs of a "witch's-mark,". They also used sleep deprivation, which broke the accused's spirits to make them more susceptible to confession. They extracted many confessions using these methods, but the evidence was flimsy or fabricated and often coerced through physical and psychological torture.

They subjected the accused to a range of brutal treatments. Including being forced to confess to a range of supposed crimes, from hexing neighbors to consorting with demons. The sheer number of accused and convicted witches was staggering. The trials became a spectacle that drew crowds and further inflamed community tensions. Hopkins' investigations spread through Essex and Suffolk, where he held examinations in local churches, creating a sense of hysteria and fear that gripped the region. The Chelmsford trials marked a turning point in Hopkins' campaign. The sheer scale of the accusations and convictions left a lasting impact on the region's collective psyche. Thus, casting a shadow over the lives of countless individuals and families for generations to come.

Following the events in Chelmsford, Hopkins moved his operation to Sudbury, another town in Suffolk, where he continued his witch-hunting crusade with unrelenting fervor. Hopkins' sudden arrival surprised the people of Sudbury, still reeling from the aftermath of the Chelmsford trials. Townsfolk soon found themselves entangled in a web of accusations and suspicions.

As before, Hopkins' methods relied heavily on the use of "pricking tests" and "swimming tests" to determine guilt, which often resulted in false positives and further fueled the hysteria. Anyone suspected of "strange" or "ungodly" behavior, such as being a loner, having a disability, or exhibiting unusual behavior, was at risk of accusation. This led to a climate where neighbors, friends, and even family members were fearful of being implicated.

The atmosphere in Sudbury became increasingly tense, with people living in constant fear of being accused and facing the same brutal treatment as those in Chelmsford. As the accusations mounted, the community became increasingly divided. Some people turning against their own loved ones to avoid being accused themselves. The Sudbury trials further showed how Hopkins' methods could quickly escalate into mass hysteria, leaving a trail of destruction and devastation in their wake.

Hopkins' activities continued unabated in Sudbury, with his witch-hunting crusade showing no signs of slowing down, until growing criticism from religious leaders and local magistrates eroded his influence. The once-zealous support for Hopkins' methods waned as clergymen and skeptics started questioning the legitimacy of his practices, citing concerns about the use of dubious evidence and the treatment of those accused. Not only did the local community criticize Hopkins, but news of his actions spread to other parts of the country, prompting scrutiny from those who had initially supported him.

By 1647, Hopkins had generated enough opposition that his critics forced him to defend his practices publicly, so he published a pamphlet titled *The Discovery of Witches*. In it, he attempted to justify his actions and distance himself from accusations of cruelty and impropriety, but his efforts only seemed to further polarize the debate. Hopkins' pamphlet was a desperate attempt to salvage his reputation and maintain his grip on the witch-hunting frenzy. But it ultimately failed to silence his critics, who continued to question the validity of his methods and the morality of his actions.

As the fervor of his early successes waned, Hopkins faced increasing opposition. Allegations of financial exploitation and abuse of power mounted. Critics began accusing him of exploiting public fear for personal gain. Towns that had once welcomed him were now weary of his presence and the violence and disruption that accompanied his witch-hunting operations.

Hopkins' witch-hunting campaign had a devastating impact on the communities he visited. Historians estimate that Hopkins' career ended after he killed over 200 people. This is a staggering number, considering the English witch trials were generally less lethal than those in continental Europe. His methods caused irreversible harm, not only through the lives lost but also through the mistrust and trauma his actions sowed within communities.

Hopkins' methods set a dangerous precedent for future witch-hunters, normalizing the use of torture and dubious means to gather evidence in England. His brutal techniques and public trials fueled the myth of witches as malevolent, ever-present threats. His techniques later influenced trials in the American colonies, where witchcraft accusations similarly erupted in feverish, violent episodes. Hopkins' campaign shows individuals can weaponize societal paranoia for profit and influence when exacerbated by turbulent times.

Matthew Hopkins' legacy as the "Witchfinder General" undoubtedly left an indelible mark on English history. It shaped the nation's witch-hunting practices and left a legacy of brutality and fear. Through pricking, the swimming test, and psychological torment, Hopkins became England's most infamous witch-hunter, embodying the dangerous blend of zealotry, greed, and cruelty. His methods and the mass hysteria he fueled left a profound impact on the communities he targeted. Many of which would never fully recover from the trauma of his witch-hunting campaigns.

CHAPTER 6
SCHERER, REMY, AND WITCH-HUNTING HYSTERIA

Figures like Georg Scherer and Nicholas Remy are emblematic of the extremities to which individuals in positions of power and influence will go to eradicate perceived threats posed by witches. Both men were instrumental in the witch-hunting hysteria of their time. They leveraged their positions to incite fear, spread accusations, and advocate for brutal methods of persecution, torture, and execution. Though operating in different regions of Europe, Scherer in Austria and Remy in Lorraine, France, both shared a common zeal for the eradication of witches. Their actions contributed to some of the most tragic and extensive witch-hunts in European history.

Georg Scherer

In his position as an Austrian Jesuit preacher, Scherer wielded significant influence over the religious and secular communities of the region. His fiery sermons, filled with dire warnings about the dangers of witchcraft, played a major role in stirring up public fears. He argued witches were in league with the

Devil and that their actions brought catastrophe upon communities. Scherer's writings, speeches, and public denunciations of witches acted as a catalyst for local witch-hunts. It was his ability to stir up fear and religious fervor that made him a key figure in the witch-hunting movement.

Scherer delivered impassioned sermons across Austria and southern Germany, particularly in regions where the Catholic Church was facing pressure from Protestant influences. In his sermons, he proclaimed witches were in league with Satan. He described them as perpetrators of many misfortunes, including storms, disease outbreaks, and failed harvests. By attributing these calamities to witchcraft, Scherer framed witches as not only religious enemies but also as serious threats to the well-being of the community. His sermons frequently featured graphic descriptions of the supposed crimes committed by witches, further inflaming public fears.

Through his sermons, Scherer spread the idea that townsfolk should expose suspected witches in public spectacles, where the community would publicly condemn and shame them. These public condemnations and the following witch trials provided the community with an opportunity to punish those believed to be involved with satanic practices. Scherer's rhetoric was uncompromising in its call for ruthless justice. He viewed the execution of witches as a moral duty, and anyone suspected of being a witch was to be treated as a dangerous enemy of society.

Scherer's rhetorical approach capitalized on the anxieties of the time. Economic hardship, religious tensions, and periodic outbreaks of plague marked the late 1500s. All of this contributed to an environment ripe for scapegoating. Scherer seized upon these conditions, linking witches to every conceivable misfortune, positioning them as enemies of both society and God. Scherer carefully crafted his messages to be memorable and provocative, ensuring that his audience would leave with a lasting impression of the dangers he described.

To maximize his influence, Scherer often delivered these sermons in town squares and large gatherings, where he could reach hundreds of people at once. His sermons were not just about spreading religious doctrine but theatrical events that dramatized the threat of witchcraft and created a heightened sense of urgency among listeners. By using language that was both vivid and accusatory, Scherer pushed the boundaries of what was socially acceptable. Instilling a palpable fear that witches were present within their very communities. In this sense, Scherer was one of the early propagandists for witch-hunting, turning it into a communal duty to identify and root out suspected witches.

Unlike some religious figures who merely endorsed witch-hunting from afar, Scherer actively encouraged the use of torture and public trials. He believed that torture was an effective means to uncover hidden witches and force confessions from those who might otherwise refuse to admit their crimes. Scherer's endorsement of torture was influential because townsfolk considered him a spiritual authority. His approval gave secular authorities a form of religious justification for their actions, thus legitimizing the use of brutal methods.

People often called Scherer's sermons "spectacle justice," where he publicly condemned and punished suspected witches. Scherer believed public trials would strongly discourage others from practicing witchcraft. He believed public punishments served as moral lessons. Scherer thought dramatic public executions would strengthen his teachings and show that witchcraft wasn't acceptable. He would often be present at these trials, lending his voice to the accusations and ensuring that his messages reached those assembled to witness the proceedings.

Where public trials led to executions, Scherer would preach directly to the condemned, treating their deaths as a necessary sacrifice for the purification of society. This participation in the proceedings further reinforced his image as a "spiritual warrior" against the forces of darkness. However, his involvement also heightened the brutality of the trials, as his religious authority made it difficult for anyone to question the legality or morality of the methods used. Many times, Scherer's influence led to harsher sentences and the extension of torture as a standard practice in the witch trials within the regions he affected.

Scherer waged a psychological war against communities by embedding his sermons with the threat of the demonic. He created an atmosphere where suspicion and mistrust permeated social relationships. This climate of fear made communities increasingly likely to report suspected witches. This led to an explosion of accusations and arrests in Austria and Bavaria. Friends turned against friends, neighbors against neighbors, and even family members became suspects.

Scherer frequently emphasized that witches were skilled at hiding in plain sight. He suggested that anyone in the community could be secretly engaged in witchcraft. This tactic effectively amplified public paranoia, creating a sense that no one was safe, and that vigilance was essential. He suggested that signs of misfortune, such as sick livestock or spoiled crops, were evidence of witchcraft. This prompted the townsfolk to see ordinary misfortunes as proof of supernatural malice. This reasoning paved the way for accusations based on circumstantial evidence, often leading to tragic outcomes for innocent people.

His sermons also called for community vigilance, urging townsfolk to report any unusual behavior they might see as a sign of witchcraft. This created a culture of suspicion that made it easy for personal vendettas and grudges to be resolved through witchcraft accusations. Scherer thus weaponized communal fears, transforming the simple act of reporting a neighbor into a moral duty. This "vigilante" aspect of witch-hunting was devastating, as it led to countless false accusations and executions.

Nicholas Remy

Nicholas Remy was a devout Catholic and a staunch believer in the existence of witches. He believed a witch killed his son. He rose to prominence as a notorious judge in Lorraine, a region in eastern France that was deeply entrenched in the witch-hunts of the late 16th century. Remy's unwavering conviction in the existence of witches, whom he viewed as dangerous heretics and servants of the Devil, drove his zealous pursuit of those accused of witchcraft. His position as a magistrate granted him the authority to oversee witch trials, and he quickly gained a reputation as one of the most fervent witch-hunters in Europe.

He held a deep-seated conviction that they posed a significant threat to the Catholic Church and the social order. This fueled Remy's fervor for rooting witches out. He believed witches handled a wide range of evils, from crop failures and illnesses to unexplained events and natural disasters. As a result, he saw it as his duty to identify and prosecute those suspected of witchcraft, often using dubious methods and questionable evidence to secure convictions. A lack of due process and a disregard for the rights of the accused marked Remy's methods. He prioritized the pursuit of witches over protecting the innocent.

Remy's reputation as a witch-hunter spread far and wide. He drew attention from other European countries that earned him a place among the most feared and reviled figures of the time. Remy's belief in witchcraft was so intense that he came to regard it as the most destructive threat to society. He saw his role as a judge, both a religious duty and a means of purging the community of evil. Remy's most significant contribution to the witch-hunting movement was his active involvement in trials, which resulted in hundreds of executions. Over the course of his career, Remy oversaw the execution of over 800 individuals accused of witchcraft, making him one of the most infamous witch-hunting figures of his time.

In 1595, Remy published his treatise *Demonolatry* (*La Démonolâtrie*), in which he outlined his beliefs about witchcraft and the methods of identifying witches. This book would have a significant impact on the witch-hunting practices in France and beyond, further cementing Remy's legacy as a fervent and influential figure in the witch trials.

A ruthless disregard for the wellbeing of the accused marked Nicholas Remy's methods of extracting confessions from the accused witches. He held a firm conviction that torture was an essential tool in uncovering the truth of witchcraft. Like many of his contemporaries, Remy believed that physical violence was a necessary step in the judicial process, and he was unapologetic in his use of torture to extract confessions. He was fond of the most brutal forms of torture, including the rack and strappado, which were designed to break the body and spirit of the accused. The rack, a device that stretched the victim's limbs to the point of dislocation, was a favorite of Remy's. This method of torture allowed him to extract confessions through a combination of physical pain and psychological intimidation.

Besides physical torture, Remy's methods also included psychological intimidation. This type of intimidation was used to break the will of the accused and extract confessions. He would frequently use threats of execution, public humiliation, and the destruction of the accused's reputation as leverage to force confessions. Remy would often manipulate the accused psychologically, telling them there would be no execution if they confessed, or he would spare their families if they cooperated. He designed these antics to erode the accused's sense of self and their will to resist, making them more susceptible to false confessions. He then used the extracted confessions as evidence in trials to convict others. This would then create a self-reinforcing cycle of persecution. These confessions, often fabricated under duress, would then justify further arrests and executions, expanding the reach of the witch-hunts.

Remy's firm belief in the reality of witchcraft meant he had little regard for the possibility of false accusations or the innocence of those he condemned. Remy believed anyone accused of witchcraft was automatically guilty, and he accepted all confessions, even if made under duress. He considered these confessions as undeniable proof of the accused's guilt. This lack of skepticism and reliance on forced confessions were major contributing factors to the scale of the witch-hunts in Lorraine during his tenure. Remy's methods were a perfectly combined use of psychological manipulation, physical torture, and a deep-seated conviction in the existence of witchcraft. Creating a culture of fear and paranoia that swept through the region, leaving a trail of destruction and death in its wake.

Nicholas Remy's beliefs about witchcraft were extreme, even for his time. He subscribed to the notion that witches were in direct communication with the Devil. This made them responsible for a wide range of social and natural calamities, from crop failures to outbreaks of disease. Remy believed witches could cause storms, summon demons, and even kill children through their supernatural powers.

In his writings and public speeches, Remy emphasized the destructive potential of witches. He portrayed them as a dangerous and insidious threat to both the physical and spiritual well-being of society. He argued that witchcraft was not merely a personal crime but a societal catastrophe, and that it was the duty of the state and church to eradicate it completely. This unwavering belief in the total evil of witches fueled his actions and influenced the severity of the witch-hunts in Lorraine.

Remy's fervor for the witch-hunts had a profound impact on the public perception of witches. His role as a magistrate lent credibility to his accusations and methods, and both church and civic authorities often supported his actions. The witch-hunts in Lorraine, under Remy's supervision, became increasingly intense, and accusations of witchcraft spread like wildfire, fueled by the judge's unshakable belief in the reality of witches.

His work contributed to the broader climate of fear and superstition that permeated Europe. Panic gripped communities in Lorraine and neighboring regions as accusations of witchcraft grew ever more common. Remy's witch-hunting was not an isolated event but part of the larger European trend where people viewed witchcraft as a constant threat that needed to be eradicated at all costs.

Georg Scherer and Nicholas Remy's legacies are deeply connected to the brutality and hysteria of the European witch-hunts. Their tireless advocacy for the prosecution and execution of witches contributed to the widespread fear that led to the deaths of thousands of individuals across Europe. Scherer's role in inciting public witch-hunts and Remy's ruthless prosecutions through torture and confessions showed the broader witch-hunting mindset of the era. A mindset that saw the eradication of witchcraft as an urgent and sacred duty.

However, as the Enlightenment took hold in the 17th century, the brutal methods employed by Scherer and Remy became increasingly criticized. Public opinion shifted, and the once-accepted practices of torture and execution became seen as both cruel and inhumane. Both Scherer and Remy's methods were called into question, and their actions ultimately became symbols of the dangers of unchecked religious fervor and judicial cruelty.

CHAPTER 7
PIERRE DE LANCRE AND BALTHASAR VON DERNBACH

Individuals whose influence and actions left indelible scars on the communities they touched mark the historical trajectory of the witch-hunts. Two such figures, Pierre de Lancre and Balthasar von Dernbach, operated in different regions of Europe yet shared a ruthless dedication to eradicating perceived witchcraft. Their roles as agents of persecution illuminate the interconnected dynamics of fear, authority, and religious fervor that characterized the European witch-hunts.

Pierre de Lancre

Pierre de Lancre was a French inquisitor, magistrate and judge. He was one of the most infamous figures of the early 17th century because of his pivotal role in the Basque witch trials. Appointed by King Henry IV of France to investigate alleged witchcraft in the Labourd region, de Lancre unleashed a campaign of terror. His reign resulted in hundreds of arrests and just as many executions.

The turbulent religious and social climate of his era profoundly shaped De Lancre, particularly the Catholic-Protestant struggles that defined post-Reformation Europe. As a staunch Catholic, he viewed witchcraft not merely as a criminal act, but as a profound spiritual threat to the established social and religious order. This notion was deeply ingrained in his worldview. His commission in the Basque region coincided with widespread unrest and suspicions of heresy, which de Lancre sought to suppress under the guise of rooting out witches. He believed this justified the extraordinary measures he employed during his investigations.

The Basque region's unique cultural practices, including its long-standing traditions of folk magick and its matriarchal social structures, likely heightened de Lancre's suspicions. Thus, reinforcing his perception of the region as a hotbed of deviance. To him, the region's customs were evidence of deviance and an affront to Catholic orthodoxy. This notion was further fueled by the region's historical resistance to Catholicism. The cultural difference provided a convenient justification for de Lancre's actions. This allowed him to cast a wide net in his search for witches and to employ methods that were both brutal and inhumane.

The prevailing intellectual and cultural currents of his time also shaped De Lancre's views on witchcraft. Including the rise of demonology and the growing fascination with the supernatural. The writings of prominent demonologists, such as Jean Bodin, who had helped to popularize the idea of witchcraft as a global conspiracy influenced his work. De Lancre's own writings on the subject reflect this influence, as he describes witches as agents of the Devil, working to undermine the established social and religious order.

In the Basque region, a series of show trials and mass executions marked de Lancre's investigations. This was his way of rooting out what he saw as a widespread conspiracy of witches. His methods were often brutal, involving the use of torture and other forms of coercion to extract confessions from suspects. De Lancre and his allies often predetermined the outcome of these investigations, using the trials as an opportunity to settle old scores. They also provided a means to eliminate the perceived enemies of the Catholic Church. The legacy of de Lancre's work in the Basque region is a dark and troubled one, marked by widespread suffering and injustice.

De Lancre's methods during the witch-hunts maximized fear and submission among the population. He focused on creating an atmosphere of terror and uncertainty. He relied heavily on public trials and spectacular executions, often burning accused witches at the stake in full view of the townsfolk. These events served as a stark reminder of the consequences of defying the established social and religious order. And it helped to reinforce de Lancre's authority as a judge and a defender of the faith.

The trials themselves were notorious for the use of torture to extract confessions, with many accused individuals implicating others under duress. The accusations and arrests escalated as the hysteria surrounding the witch-hunts spread, implicating more and more people. Methods employed by de Lancre and his allies were often brutal, involving the use of thumbscrews, pincers, and other instruments of torture to extract confessions from suspects.

In his notorious treatise, *Tableau de l'inconstance des mauvais anges et démons (Tableau of the Inconstancy of Wicked Angels and Demons)*, de Lancre described witches as agents of chaos. He claimed they attended sabbats, consorted with demons, and sought to undermine societal order. His vivid and often lurid depictions of these supposed gatherings reinforced public fear and provided justification for the extreme measures he employed. De Lancre's descriptions of sabbats included fantastical elements, such as sexual rituals, pacts with the Devil, and the consumption of human flesh.

De Lancre claimed to have identified many signs of witchcraft, including malformed animals, unusual weather patterns, and inexplicable illnesses. All of these he attributed to the evil workings of local witches. These supposed signs were often based on superstitions and misconceptions about the natural world and served as a convenient justification for de Lancre's campaign of persecution.

Like so many others, de Lancre's trials disproportionately targeted women, particularly widows, healers, and women who were economically or socially vulnerable. He believed in the inherent moral weakness of women. This and his view of the Basque people as inherently susceptible to diabolic influence created a perfect storm of prejudice that fueled his campaign of persecution. This targeting of women was not unique to de Lancre's trials. Early modern witch-hunts disproportionately targeted women, who were seen as more vulnerable to the Devil's influence.

The legacy of de Lancre's work in the Basque region is a dark and troubled one, marked by widespread suffering and injustice. De Lancre's campaign in the Basque region resulted in the execution of at least 70 individuals. With some historians estimating the total number of his victims ranging much higher when considering the broader impact of his witch-hunting rhetoric. His methods left a lasting legacy of fear and division in the region, and his writings continued to influence witch-hunting practices long after his death.

Balthasar von Dernbach

Pierre de Lancre may have limited his persecutions to France. But Balthasar von Dernbach, the Prince-Abbot of Fulda in Germany, directed one of the most infamous witch-hunting campaigns in the Holy Roman Empire. His tenure as abbot was a relentless pursuit of witches, motivated by both religious conviction and political ambition.

Balthasar von Dernbach rose to prominence during the tumultuous Counter-Reformation. This period marked an intense Catholic renewal and opposition to Protestantism that swept across Europe in the 16th century. As the Prince-Abbot of Fulda, which was both a powerful and influential position, von Dernbach wielded significant authority over the region. He accomplished this by combining his spiritual leadership with secular power. This unique blend of roles allowed him to shape the fate of Fulda. This was a region that had seen significant Protestant influence. He used his position to merge Catholic authority in the face of growing dissent.

Von Dernbach sought to reinforce Catholic orthodoxy and suppress any challenges to his authority which were deeply intertwined with his witch-hunting efforts. His motivations were not purely spiritual; they also had a strategic dimension. By purging the region of perceived witches, he aimed to create a climate of fear and submission, solidifying his grip on power and maintaining the Catholic dominance in Fulda. He had a firm belief in the pervasive threat of witchcraft. Fueled by the prevailing superstitions and fears of the time, combined with his political aspirations, he created a volatile environment in which accusations of witchcraft could flourish.

As the Prince-Abbot of Fulda, von Dernbach was well-positioned to exploit the fears and anxieties of his subjects while using the witch-hunting craze to further his own ambitions. His actions were part of a broader campaign to suppress Protestantism and maintain Catholic control in the region. He appeared willing to use any means necessary to achieve his goals. The witch-hunting frenzy that swept through Fulda during his tenure was a testament to his effectiveness in exploiting the fears and superstitions of his subjects. However, it ultimately contributed to the consolidation of Catholic power in the region.

A ruthless determination to root out perceived witches marked Von Dernbach's witch-hunting campaign, and it relied heavily on intimidation and torture to elicit confessions. He appointed Balthasar Nuss, an equally zealous figure, as his chief witch-hunter. Together, they orchestrated a campaign that was characterized by brutal interrogations and systematic executions. The methods employed by von Dernbach and Nuss broke the spirits of those accused, and they included some of the most gruesome and inhumane techniques of the time.

Torture chambers were a key component of von Dernbach's campaign, and he subjected suspected witches to physical and psychological torment in these facilities. The rack, thumbscrews, and other implements designed to inflict maximum pain were used to extract confessions. These methods often left the victims with permanent physical and emotional scars. Public executions were also a favorite tactic of von Dernbach, as he sought to instill fear and show the power of his authority. Von Dernbach often held these spectacles in the town square, serving as a stark reminder of the consequences of being accused of witchcraft.

Besides torture and public executions, von Dernbach's campaign also relied on forced confessions to implicate others and create a network of accusations that spread throughout the region. This was a classic example of the "witch-hunt" mentality, where accusations were used to fuel further accusations. The accused often named others to avoid further torture or execution. The focus on confession, regardless of its source, drew many innocent people into the witch-hunt frenzy. To avoid a worse fate, witch-hunters often forced individuals to confess to crimes they didn't commit.

Von Dernbach's campaign was notable for its disregard for due process, and accusations were often based on hearsay or flimsy evidence. Von Dernbach's campaign rarely allowed those arrested to escape conviction, and often denied the accused a fair trial or the opportunity to defend themselves. The entire process was swift and merciless, with the goal of eliminating perceived witches from the community quickly and efficiently.

The witch-hunts orchestrated by Balthasar von Dernbach reached their peak in the late 16th century, resulting in the tragic deaths of over 200 individuals. The Fulda Witch Trials, as they came to be known, had a profound and lasting impact on the local population. These trials sowed a deep mistrust within communities and left a scar that would take centuries to heal. Von Dernbach primarily targeted women in his campaign, but he also accused and executed men and children, highlighting the brutal and indiscriminate nature of the witch-hunts.

The economic and social consequences of von Dernbach's witch-hunts were severe and far-reaching. These witch-hunts tore families apart as von Dernbach accused, arrested, and executed their loved ones, leaving behind a trail of devastation and heartbreak. The witch-hunts disrupted trade and commerce, causing people to lose their livelihoods. This climate of fear stifled community life, making it difficult for townsfolk to trust one another or engage in everyday activities.

Even after von Dernbach's death, the scars of his campaign lingered, shaping the region's history for decades to come. The witch-hunts had a lasting impact on the social and economic structures of the community. And it would take generations for the region to recover from the trauma inflicted by von Dernbach's brutal campaign.

While Pierre de Lancre and Balthasar von Dernbach operated in different regions and contexts, their actions shared common features that highlight the similarities between their witch-hunting campaigns. Both men leveraged their authority to instill fear and suppress dissent, using their positions of power to manipulate and control the populations under their jurisdiction. This was a deliberate strategy, designed to create a climate of terror and submission that would allow them to maintain their grip on power.

Both de Lancre and von Dernbach targeted vulnerable townsfolk, particularly women, under the guise of combating witchcraft. Women were easy targets, often because of their social and economic status. Flimsy evidence or hearsay frequently led to accusations of witchcraft against them. This was a classic example of the "witch-hunt" mentality, where witch-hunters scapegoated women for societal problems and used them to exert control over the community. By targeting women, de Lancre and von Dernbach could create a sense of fear and mistrust that would allow them to maintain their power and influence.

Both de Lancre and von Dernbach used public trials and executions as tools of intimidation, ensuring that their campaigns left a lasting impact on the communities they terrorized. Public trials were a key component of their strategy, as they allowed de Lancre and von Dernbach to showcase their power and authority to the community. Using public executions was also a deliberate tactic, designed to create a sense of fear and dread that would prevent others from speaking out against them. By using these tactics, de Lancre and von Dernbach could create a culture of fear and submission. This would allow them to maintain their grip on power for years to come.

CHAPTER 8
MICHAELIS AND CADDELL IN THE WITCH-HUNT ERA

The history of witch-hunting is a complex and disturbing chapter in human history. There was the involvement of various figures who employed their positions and skills to identify marks, interrogate, and prosecute alleged witches. Among them were Sebastian Michaelis, a French inquisitor and theologian whose writings and methods contributed significantly to the religious framing of witchcraft. Michaelis was a prominent figure in the Catholic Church during the 17th century, and his works on demonology and witchcraft helped to solidify the Church's stance on the matter. His writings often emphasized the idea that witches were in league with the Devil, and their supposed powers were a manifestation of their pact with evil. This framing of witchcraft as a religious issue rather than a medical or social one helped to fuel the witch-hunting fervor that swept across Europe during this time.

Another figure who played a significant role in the perpetuation of witch-hunting practices was Christian Caddell. She was a Scottish woman who assumed the guise of a "witch-pricker" to assist in one of the most peculiar and brutal methods of identifying witches. The practice of "pricking" involved using a needle to search for a witch's supposed "devil's mark." Many claimed any physical blemish or imperfection to be a sign of their pact with the Devil. Although Caddell was a woman, she was able to assume a position of authority and power by playing the part of a man.

Despite differences in their roles, both Michaelis and Caddell played significant parts in the perpetuation of witch-hunting practices. Their involvement highlights the complex and multifaceted nature of the witch-hunting phenomenon. Not only involving the actions of individual figures but also the broader social, cultural, and economic contexts in which they operated.

Sebastian Michaelis

Sebastian Michaelis was a Dominican friar, inquisitor, and theologian whose work during the height of the European witch-hunts profoundly influenced the understanding and prosecution of witchcraft in early modern France. His writings, particularly his widely read *Histoire admirable de la possession d'une penitente* (*The Admirable History of a Possessed Penitent*), combined theological arguments with sensational accounts of demonic possession and witchcraft, helping to perpetuate fear and suspicion across Europe.

Michaelis was born into a period of profound religious upheaval, a time when the very foundations of Christianity were being challenged and redefined. The Protestant Reformation, which began in the early 16th century, had fragmented the Christian church, creating deep divisions between

Catholics and Protestants. The Catholic Church, determined to maintain its authority and suppress the growing heretical movements, responded with the Counter-Reformation. A concerted effort to reclaim religious dominance and restore the Church's influence. Witchcraft, often linked to heresy and seen as a direct affront to God's authority, became a focal point for this crackdown. The Church viewed it as a manifestation of the Devil's work, a perversion of the natural order that threatened the very fabric of society.

It was within this tumultuous context that Michaelis joined the Dominican Order, an institution with a long history of theological scholarship and involvement in the Inquisition. The Dominicans fiercely defended Catholic orthodoxy, often acting as inquisitors in cases of heresy and witchcraft. Their role was to root out perceived threats to the faith, using a combination of theological rigor and emotional appeal to persuade individuals to renounce their heretical views. Michaelis' own religious training emphasized the use of reason and theological scholarship, but his work as an inquisitor also revealed a more sensational and emotional side. Michaelis gravitated towards the dramatic and often lurid aspects of combating perceived threats to the faith. He used the spectacle of witch trials and inquisitions to galvanize public opinion and reinforce the Church's authority. This approach, while effective in terms of public relations, also contributed to the increasingly hysterical and violent atmosphere surrounding witch-hunting, as the boundaries between reason and superstition blurred.

Michaelis gained prominence for his involvement in one of the most infamous cases of demonic possession in France: the Aix-en-Provence possession case of 1610. This case revolved around Madeleine de Demandolx de la Palud, a young and devout Ursuline nun who displayed symptoms of possession. These included violent fits, speaking in tongues, and accusing others of witchcraft. The convent, once a sanctuary of peace and contemplation, was now a hotbed of chaos and fear, as the nun's behavior became increasingly erratic and disturbing. The Church appointed Michaelis to investigate and oversee the case, because his role as an inquisitor put him in direct contact with the alleged demonic forces. As he delved deeper into the case, he became convinced that the forces of darkness were at work, and that the nun's possession was a manifestation of the Devil's power.

The investigation unfolded in a highly charged atmosphere, as accusations spread beyond the convent to members of the local community. The air was thick with suspicion and fear, as townsfolk pointed fingers and accused one another of witchcraft. Michaelis' presence only added to the tension as he conducted his inquiry with a sense of urgency and conviction. His methods combined theological interrogation with reliance on physical evidence, such as the identification of "witchmarks" or other signs of diabolic influence. He also used torture, a common practice in witch trials, to extract confessions from the accused. Using torture was a brutal and inhumane practice, but one that was widely accepted as a necessary tool in pursuing truth and justice. Michaelis' questions often centered on the accused's interactions with the Devil, participation in sabbats (gatherings of witches), and acts of maleficium (harmful magick). The confessions gained under duress often included elaborate and horrifying details of demonic pacts and rituals, reinforcing public fears and justifying further persecution.

The case resulted in multiple arrests and executions, including that of a priest, Louis Gaufridi, who they accused of being a sorcerer and having seduced Madeleine into witchcraft. His trial was a spectacle of drama and horror as they publicly humiliated and tortured the accused. They burned the priest at the stake in the public square, surrounded by a jeering crowd, in a gruesome execution. The case was a stark reminder of the dangers of witchcraft and the importance of vigilance in the face of demonic threats. Michaelis' role in the case cemented his reputation as a leading expert on witchcraft and demonic possession. Whereby he continued to play a prominent role in the witch-hunting efforts of the Catholic Church.

Sebastian Michaelis documented the Aix-en-Provence case and his broader beliefs about witchcraft and possession in his book, *Histoire admirable de la possession d'une penitente*. Published in 1612, this work became one of the most influential accounts of demonic possession and witchcraft in early modern Europe. It shaped the public's perception of these phenomena and provided a practical guide for identifying and prosecuting witches. The book's impact was far-reaching, influencing not only the Catholic Church's witch-hunting efforts but also the broader cultural and social landscape of Europe.

In the *Histoire admirable*, Michaelis described possession as a direct intervention by the Devil to undermine Christian society. He detailed Madeleine's symptoms, including her supernatural knowledge and aversion to holy objects, as evidence of the Devil's influence. By framing possession as a spiritual battle, Michaelis emphasized the necessity of diligently prosecuting witches, considering them the Devil's earthly agents. This perspective legitimized the witch-hunting efforts of the Catholic Church, which viewed witches as a threat to the very fabric of society. Michaelis' account of Madeleine's possession was a masterful blend of theological argumentation and dramatic narrative. This captured the public's imagination and reinforcing the notion that witches were a real and present danger.

Michaelis portrayed witches as willing participants in the Devil's schemes, attending sabbats, engaging in blasphemous rites, and spreading chaos through evil deeds and harmful magick. He argued that witches often targeted vulnerable individuals, including children and the sick, further heightening the sense of danger they posed. This portrayal of witches as malevolent agents of the Devil reinforced the need for strict prosecution and punishment. This also contributed to the widespread acceptance of witch-hunting as a necessary measure to protect society. By framing witches as a threat to the social order, Michaelis' book helped to create a climate of fear and hysteria that fueled the witch-hunting frenzy of the time.

The *Histoire admirable* also justified the use of torture as a necessary tool for uncovering the truth about witchcraft. Michaelis believed that witches, under the Devil's influence, would lie and deny their guilt unless subjected to physical and psychological pressure. This perspective legitimized the brutal methods employed during the witch trials and contributed to the widespread acceptance of torture as a judicial practice. Using torture was a brutal and inhumane practice, but one that was widely accepted as a necessary tool in pursuing truth and justice. Michaelis' book served as a practical guide for inquisitors, providing them with a theological justification for the use of torture and a framework for identifying and prosecuting witches.

One of Sebastian Michaelis's most notorious contributions to the practice of witch-hunting was his development of the "Devil's interrogation." This method was based on the belief that witches and the possessed were under the Devil's control and would therefore require extraordinary measures to reveal the truth. Michaelis believed that the Devil's influence was a tangible, physical force. Therefore, he thought holy objects, physical torture, and psychological manipulation could counter it. He believed that by subjecting the accused to intense suffering, he could break their resistance and free their souls from the Devil's grasp.

The Devil's interrogation typically involved a combination of leading theological questions designed to trap the accused in contradictions. It used holy objects to provoke reactions, and physical and psychological torture to break the accused's resistance. Methods included the rack, thumbscrews, and sleep deprivation, all of which inflicted maximum pain and discomfort on the accused. Michaelis viewed these techniques as spiritually justified, believing that the torment inflicted on the body would ultimately lead to the liberation of the soul. However, modern historians recognize that these methods often led to false confessions, as the accused sought to end their suffering by saying whatever their interrogators wanted to hear.

Even in his own time, people did not universally accept Michaelis's methods and conclusions. Some critics within the Church and secular authorities questioned the validity of evidence received through torture and complained about the potential for abuse. The Aix-en-Provence case, in particular, drew scrutiny because of the sensational nature of the accusations and the lack of concrete evidence. Many viewed the case as a prime example of the dangers of witch-hunting, where superstition and hysteria, not facts, fueled the accusations. Despite these criticisms, Michaelis's work remained influential, as it aligned with the broader Counter-Reformation emphasis on combating heresy and reinforcing Catholic orthodoxy.

The Devil's interrogation was a hallmark of Michaelis' approach to witch-hunting, and it was used to significant effect many times. However, this interrogation method also resulted in many miscarriages of justice, as the Devil's interrogation tortured innocent people and forced them to confess to crimes they did not commit.

Christian Caddell

Christian Caddell was a Scottish woman who operated under the alias John Dickson. She left an indelible mark on the tumultuous history of 17th-century Scotland. Witch trials ravaged the country during this period. The trials fueled a toxic mix of religious zeal and political instability. It was amidst this backdrop of fear and superstition that Caddell emerged as a "witch-pricker," a role that would cement her infamy in the annals of history.

Witch-pricking was a dubious method employed to identify witches, was based on the misguided belief that they bore a "witch's-mark" that rendered them impervious to pain. This notion, rooted in medieval folklore, was used to justify the use of torture and other forms of coercion to extract confessions from accused witches. Caddell's involvement in this practice highlights the unique and often bizarre methods employed to root out supposed witches. It underscored the depths of human depravity and the dangers of unchecked fear and superstition.

Caddell's decision to disguise herself as a man and adopting the alias John Dickson was likely driven by the limited opportunities available to women during this time. Because society confined women to domestic roles and made them scapegoats during this time. Caddell's decision to present herself as a man enabled her to take on the lucrative and influential role of witch-pricker. By doing this, she could exploit societal fears for personal gain. This calculated move not only speaks to the societal constraints faced by women but also to the cunning and ambition that drove Caddell to succeed in a male-dominated world.

As a witch-pricker, Caddell's actions were a testament to the complexities of gender and power within the context of witch-hunts. Caddell's resourcefulness and determination were clear as she navigated the treacherous landscape of 17th-century Scotland, where women faced marginalization and oppression. While her actions were undoubtedly reprehensible, Caddell's story serves as a reminder of the darker aspects of human nature and the dangers of unchecked power and fear.

Caddell, like other witch-prickers, likely employed trickery to ensure her findings aligned with the accusations. Specially crafted retractable needles allowed prickers to create the illusion of painless pricking, providing "evidence" of a witch's-mark. The overwhelming fear and hysteria surrounding witchcraft at the time made townsfolk rarely question these deceptions.

A trail of exploitation and false accusations marked Christian Caddell's career as a witch-pricker, leaving a devastating legacy of innocent lives lost and shattered families. Her actions, fueled by a desire for power and financial gain, led to the arrest and execution of many individuals, many of whom were innocent and blameless. She manipulated and deceived the very people she was supposed to help, the accused witches, forcing them to endure the agony of torture and the terror of false accusations.

As a witch-pricker, Caddell's role was to identify those bearing the supposed "witch's-mark," a notion that was as baseless as it was brutal. However, Caddell didn't just identify suspected witches; she actively took part in the persecution of those she deemed "witches," using her position of power to orchestrate their downfall. The consequences of her actions were catastrophic, as the very system that was supposed to protect them tore apart innocent lives.

However, Caddell's deception was eventually uncovered, and her own downfall was swift and merciless. Her trial was a stark contrast to the kangaroo courts she had once presided over and exposed the full extent of Caddell's crimes. The court held her accountable for her role in perpetuating the witch-hunts. She confessed to using a method of identifying witches by looking into their eyes, which was considered witchcraft. The court condemned Christian to forced labor on Barbados's fever-ravaged plantations, though she avoided execution. Notably, they transported her on the same day they burned her last victims at the stake. Estimates suggest she may have been responsible for the deaths of 6-10 innocent people. The exposure of her fraud cast a long shadow over the practice of witch-pricking. Again, highlighting the dangers of unchecked power and the devastating consequences of allowing superstition and opportunism to guide our actions.

Christian Caddell's story is both unique and emblematic of the broader phenomenon of the witch-hunts. As a woman operating in a male-dominated role, she subverted societal norms even as she perpetuated the systemic persecution of other women. The way she acted and what happened to her shows how weak the methods of finding and prosecuting witches were and how humans can be both cruel and strong.

Sebastian Michaelis and Christian Caddell represent two distinct yet interconnected facets of the European witch-hunts.

Michaelis, with his theological rigor and reliance on torture, embodied the institutional and religious dimensions of persecution. While Caddell, through her role as a witch-pricker, personified the opportunistic exploitation of fear. Together, their histories illuminate the complex and often tragic interplay of belief, power, and superstition that defined this dark chapter in human history.

CHAPTER 9
THE MAGISTRATE AND THE CHIEF JUSTICE

The history of witch-hunting in England reflects a unique blend of local superstition, legal practices, and cultural anxieties that fueled the persecution of alleged witches. One of the most notable figures in this history is Roger Nowell. Nowell was a magistrate whose role in the Pendle Witch Trials of 1612 set the standard for future witch trials in England. His methods, particularly his reliance on children's testimonies and detailed investigations, shaped the conduct of English witch trials during a time of heightened fear and suspicion.

However, the history of English witch-hunting also includes figures who questioned the validity of witchcraft accusations. One of the most influential voices was Sir John Holt. Holt was a Chief Justice in England who's rational and evidence-based approach to witch trials in the late 17th century marked the beginning of the end for witch-hunting in England.

Roger Nowell

Roger Nowell served as a magistrate for the Forest of Pendle in Lancashire, an area known for its rugged terrain, isolation, and deeply entrenched superstitions. The Forest of Pendle, a vast and unforgiving expanse of moorland, was home to a tight-knit community of farmers, shepherds, and laborers who lived in small villages and hamlets. The harsh climate and limited access to the outside world contributed to a sense of self-reliance and a strong tradition of oral storytelling. These stories often blurred the lines between fact and fiction. During the reign of King James I, witchcraft was a subject of heightened attention, fueled by the King's personal interest in the topic, as shown in his book *Daemonologie* (1597). This treatise drew heavily from the works of earlier writers, such as King James VI of Scotland. It presented a comprehensive case against witchcraft, emphasizing its perceived threat to the social order and the Christian faith.

Lancashire's reputation for lawlessness and religious dissent added to the region's susceptibility to accusations of witchcraft. The county had a long history of conflict between Catholics and Protestants, and the tensions between these two groups created an atmosphere of mistrust and hostility. As a result, accusations of witchcraft often became entangled with charges of heresy and treason, making it easier for individuals to be convicted and punished. As a magistrate, Nowell was responsible for maintaining order and investigating crimes, including allegations of witchcraft.

His involvement in the trial of the Pendle witches placed him at the center of one of England's most infamous episodes of witch persecution. Nowell's role in these events has been the subject of much debate and controversy. Some historians view him as a ruthless and zealous prosecutor, while others see him as a product of his time, acting under the laws and customs of his era. The Pendle Witch Trials are among the most famous witch trials in English history. They resulted in the execution of 10 individuals and the imprisonment of at least two others. The trials are significant for the insight they provide into the intersection of local superstitions, legal practices, and broader cultural anxieties about witchcraft.

The case began in March 1612 when Alizon Device, a young woman from a family with a reputation for witchcraft, had a chance encounter with John Law, a peddler. Law accused Alizon of cursing him after he refused to sell her pins, claiming that he had subsequently fallen ill. Law's accusation started a chain reaction, leading to accusations of witchcraft against Alizon and her grandmother Elizabeth Southerns, known as the Demdike family.

The Chattoxes, their neighbors, had long regarded the Device family with suspicion. A long-standing feud embroiled between the Chattox and Device families. These tensions, combined with Nowell's intervention, escalated the situation into one of the most infamous witch trials in England.

Nowell's role in the Pendle trials was pivotal, serving as the driving force behind the investigation into the allegations of witchcraft. As the local magistrate, he conducted preliminary investigations into the claims, meticulously gathering information and testimonies from the townsfolk. Nowell interrogated Alizon Device, who confessed to cursing John Law and implicated other members of her family. However, it is essential to note that her confession was likely influenced by the intense pressure and fear she faced during her questioning. This was a common tactic used during the trials to extract confessions from accused witches.

Nowell expanded the investigation to include other suspected witches, focusing on local rumors and testimonies that had been circulating in the community. He relied on children's testimonies, particularly that of Jennet Device, Alizon's nine-year-old sister, who played a crucial role in securing convictions. Jennet's statements were critical in the trial, as she accused her own family members and others of participating in witchcraft. The court accepted her testimony, reflecting the legal system's willingness to prioritize evidence that aligned with existing suspicions, regardless of its reliability. The Pendle trials frequently relied on children's testimonies, like Jennet's, because people believed children were less vulnerable to the devil's influence. Authorities thought children were more likely to reveal accurate information about witchcraft.

This highly publicized trial took place at Lancaster Assizes in August 1612, with Sir James Altham and Sir Edward Bromley presiding over the proceedings. The judges charged the accused with a range of heinous crimes, including using harmful magick to cause illness, death, and destruction. Several key features that would ultimately contribute to the tragic outcome marked the trial.

One of the most significant aspects of the trial was the reliance on coerced confessions and testimonies. Investigators pressured the accused intensely, often leading them to make false confessions that implicated others. The testimonies of children, particularly that of Jennet Device, played a pivotal role in securing convictions. However, witch-hunters often got these testimonies through dubious means, and they lacked credibility.

The trial also exploited the community's deep-seated fear of witchcraft. Sensationalized accounts of sabbats, the alleged gatherings of witches, and demonic pacts became evidence. This approach created a sense of drama and spectacle, further fueling the townsfolk's anxiety and paranoia. Ultimately, the result was devastating with 10 people from the Device and Chattox families, declared guilty and hanged.

Roger Nowell's approach to witch-hunting was methodical, aligning with contemporary legal practices and King James I's guidelines on witchcraft, as outlined in *Daemonologie*. Nowell's interrogations extracted confessions, often through intimidation and psychological pressure. While English law prohibited the use of physical torture, the intense atmosphere, isolation and the threat of punishment likely compelled the accused to confess.

Nowell relied heavily on testimonies from children and neighbors. Jennet Device's testimony, in particular, was astonishing, as it highlighted the legal system's willingness to accept evidence from young and impressionable witnesses. Jennet Device's testimony set a precedent for future trials in England, leading to increased reliance on children's statements as evidence against accused witches.

The investigation drew on local rumors and grievances, reflecting the deeply ingrained suspicion and fear of witchcraft in Lancashire. This approach ensured that the trials resonated with the local townsfolk, who were eager to see justice served against those they believed to be witches.

Sir John Holt

Opposing the witch-hunt trend, Holt, the Lord Chief Justice, offered a rational counterpoint to figures like Nowell. Holt's judicial career spanned a time when belief in witchcraft was still widespread, but his decisions helped dismantle the legal framework that sustained the witch trials.

Born in Abingdon, Oxfordshire, in 1642, John Holt was a product of his time, yet his life's work would shape the course of English law and justice. Educated at the prestigious Gray's Inn, a renowned institution for the study of law, Holt's academic pursuits laid the foundation for his future success. In 1663, he was called to the bar, marking the beginning of a distinguished career that would span over four decades.

As a lawyer, Holt quickly rose to prominence, earning a reputation for his sharp intellect and unwavering commitment to justice. A keen sense of reason and a willingness to challenge conventional wisdom characterized his approach to the law. This mindset helped him greatly in his later years, being appointed Lord Chief Justice of the King's Bench in 1689. Holt held this esteemed position until his death in 1710, a tenure that coincided with significant social and cultural shifts in England.

The intellectual currents of the Enlightenment, which emphasized reason, skepticism, and intellectual curiosity, were challenging traditional beliefs in witchcraft and the supernatural. Holt embodied these changing attitudes, applying a rational approach to witchcraft cases that stood in stark contrast to the hysteria of earlier trials. His commitment marked an approach to evidence-based decision-making and a willingness to question established dogma. This approach not only reflected the values of the Enlightenment but also helped to shape the course of English law. This thinking paved the way for a more nuanced and informed understanding of the supernatural.

A series of significant cases marked Lord Chief Justice Holt's tenure. Each showcased his commitment to justice and his willingness to challenge conventional wisdom. His legacy extends far beyond his own time, influencing the development of English law and shaping the course of justice in the centuries that followed. Despite the challenges and controversies that surrounded him, Holt remains a figure of enduring importance. A testament to his power of reason and his enduring value of a commitment to justice.

His skepticism toward accusations of witchcraft was clear in his decisions during the many witch trials he oversaw in his career. Unlike earlier magistrates and judges, Holt required tangible evidence to support the accusations of witchcraft. He rejected hearsay, rumors, and confessions taken under duress, which had often secured convictions in earlier trials.

Holt scrutinized the testimonies of accusers, particularly those of children and neighbors. He was acutely aware of the potential for personal vendettas, envy, or fear influencing accusations, and he sought to uncover ulterior motives behind the charges. He openly questioned the validity of evidence based on supernatural claims, such as spectral evidence or physical "witch-marks" purportedly caused by witchcraft.

One of Holt's most famous decisions was in the case of Sarah Murdock in 1701. Townsfolk accused Sarah, an elderly woman from Hertfordshire, of causing illness and misfortune through witchcraft. Holt's careful questioning of the accusers revealed inconsistencies in their statements and a lack of credible evidence. He dismissed the case, stating that there was no legal basis for convicting Murdock.

He also intervened in the case of Jane Wenham in 1712, one of the last witch trials in England. Wenham, a widow accused of witchcraft, faced a trial filled with sensational accusations and dubious evidence. Holt's insistence on rational inquiry and his skepticism toward the claims led to her eventual pardon, despite widespread public pressure for her conviction.

Sir John Holt's rational approach to the witchcraft trials marked a pivotal moment in English legal history. His decisions reflected the growing influence of Enlightenment thinking and helped to delegitimize accusations of witchcraft as a basis for legal action. By requiring concrete evidence and rejecting superstitious claims, Holt effectively brought an end to the era of witch trials in England. Widespread fear, prejudice, and the brutal suppression of individuals accused of witchcraft had defined this period.

Holt's legacy is one of justice and reason, standing in stark contrast to the fear and prejudice which had dominated the earlier witch-hunting practices. His work serves as a reminder of the importance of critical thinking and the rule of law in safeguarding individual rights. Even if facing deeply ingrained cultural beliefs. The impact of his decisions was far-reaching. They not only brought an end to the witch trials but also paved the way for a more rational and evidence-based approach to justice in England.

The influence of Enlightenment thinking, which emphasized reason, individual rights, and the power of human reason, played a significant role in shaping Holt's approach to the trials. This intellectual movement, which emerged in the 17th and 18th centuries, sought to challenge traditional authority and superstition. It promoted a more rational and scientific understanding of the world. By embracing these principles, Holt brought a much-needed dose of skepticism and critical thinking to the witchcraft trials. This helped to establish a more just and fair system of justice in England.

Roger Nowell and Sir John Holt represent two distinct phases of English witch-hunting history. Nowell's role in the Pendle Witch Trials exemplifies the fear, superstition, and judicial zeal that fueled the persecution of alleged witches in the early 17th century. In contrast, Holt's rational and evidence-based approach in the late 17th and early 18th centuries helped dismantle the lack of legal framework that sustained witch trials. Which paved the way for a more enlightened and just society.

Their contrasting legacies highlight the evolution of attitudes toward witchcraft in England, reflecting broader cultural and intellectual shifts that ultimately ended the era of witch-hunting.

CHAPTER 10
ACCUSED TURNED INTO ACCUSERS

The history of the witch-hunts is rife with stories of persecution, fear, and manipulation. Though women were often the primary victims, they also played active roles in perpetuating these tragic events. Accused witches frequently found themselves in desperate situations, where accusing others became a survival mechanism. This paradoxical dynamic offers profound insights into the hierarchical, patriarchal, and deeply superstitious societies of the time.

Accusations and confessions were central to the self-perpetuating cycle of the witch trials. The accused, often tortured or coerced, would implicate others to deflect suspicion or gain leniency. These confessions were a societal spectacle, reinforcing the collective belief in witchcraft and allowing authorities to validate their actions.

Community expectations also played a significant role. Naming others as witches satisfied societal fears, made the accused appear cooperative, and temporarily provided a false sense of protection. Yet, this seldom worked as intended, because authorities eventually subjected all the implicated individuals to the same scrutiny. In deeply hierarchical societies, factional rivalries or class conflicts sometimes motivated accusations. By accusing rivals or those of higher social standing, the accused sought to regain their position within the community, a precarious and often futile endeavor.

The phenomenon of accused witches turning into accusers is a captivating aspect of the witch trials, particularly in Europe and colonial America. Accused witches often found themselves under immense pressure to confess, as most trials typically operated on the assumption of guilt. Under duress, some of the accused individuals sought to deflect blame onto others, attempting to reduce their own level of guilt or avoid harsher punishment.

This was typical, where witch-hunters tortured or harshly interrogated those accused, pushing them to name others to ease their own suffering. Authorities motivated confessions by promising leniency for implicating others, creating a perverse incentive for accused witches to cooperate. For instance, during the Salem Witch Trials, confessing witches often accused others to show their repentance and cooperation, hoping for mercy and a reduced sentence.

Accusing others could also be a means of redirecting attention and an attempt to regain some sort of social standing. In deeply hierarchical societies, accused witches might name people whose accusations could elevate their own status. Naming a rival or someone from a higher class could serve as revenge or a means of social mobility. Possibly allowing the accused to shift the focus away from their own perceived wrongdoings. These confessions reinforced the belief in witchcraft, satisfying societal fears and making the accuser appear trustworthy and cooperative.

Authorities, particularly inquisitors or magistrates, often coerced accused individuals into naming accomplices. This practice amplified the scope of the trials, allowing authorities to justify their actions and keep the cycle of accusations alive.

Isabel Gowdie

Isabel Gowdie's story stands as a unique case in Scotland's history of witch-hunts, a tale that continues to fascinate and unsettle historians to this day. In 1662, Gowdie confessed to witchcraft without coercion, offering elaborate and fantastical details that captivated and terrified the townsfolk. Her accounts painted vivid pictures of sabbats, where witches would gather to dance and make pacts with the Devil. They could fly with the aid of magickal spells, soaring through the night skies with ease. She claimed to have transformed into animals like hares and birds, using her supposed magickal powers to move undetected through the forest and fields.

Were Gowdie's confessions a lesson in storytelling, weaving a complex web of deceit and fantasy that left her audience both enthralled and appalled? Her testimony became a blueprint for questioning other accused witches. She set a grim standard for confessions that would extract similar tales of witchcraft from others. The impact of Gowdie's confessions was far-reaching, stoking fear in the region and leading to further accusations and trials. With the witch-hunting fervor intensifying, people increasingly accused others of witchcraft, often relying on flimsy evidence.

Historians continue to speculate about the motivations behind Gowdie's confessions. Some suggest she may have been driven by a mix of mental illness, religious guilt, or a bid for attention in a restrictive society. Others have proposed that she may have been a charismatic figure, using her charm and storytelling abilities to manipulate those around her. Some even claim that she told the truth. Whatever the truth may be, Gowdie's confessions had a profound impact on the witch-hunting hysteria that gripped Scotland in the 17th century. Her story exemplifies how women could wield influence, escalating witch-hunting fervor, highlighting the complex and often fraught nature of gender roles in this period.

Anna Göldi

Anna Göldi was a domestic servant who lived in 18th-century Switzerland. History remembers her as one of the last victims of Europe's witch-hunting frenzy. Her trial and execution took place in 1782, occurring long after the peak of the witch-hunts. However, it still reflected the lingering fears and deep-seated prejudices that had fueled the witch-hunting era to begin with. Göldi's tragic death highlights the devastating consequences of unfounded accusations and how they pitted women against one another in a society that offered them few other options.

At the heart of Göldi's trial was the testimony of a key accuser, the mother of the child Göldi cared for. This woman claimed that Göldi had used witchcraft to harm her child, a charge that was likely motivated by a combination of jealousy and class tensions. As a domestic servant, Göldi was vulnerable to accusations from women in higher social positions who may have seen her as a threat or a convenient scapegoat. There is no clear written documentation but, the mother's accusations were likely fueled by a desire to protect her own social status and to maintain her position within the community.

The dynamics of the Göldi case highlight the complex and often fraught relationships between women in societies that were deeply patriarchal and class-conscious. In a world where women had few economic or social opportunities, accusations of witchcraft could serve as a form of power or a survival mechanism. By leveling accusations against Göldi, the mother could deflect attention away from her own perceived shortcomings and to maintain her position within the community. This phenomenon was not unique to Göldi's case, as women throughout history have used accusations of witchcraft to assert their power or of eliminating perceived rivals.

Dame Alice Kyteler

Dame Alice Kyteler was the first women tried for witchcraft in Ireland. In the 14th century, a time of great superstition and fear, Lady Kyteler emerged as one of the earliest recorded figures in the witch trials. As a prominent Irish noblewoman, she wielded significant influence and power, which ultimately proved to be a double-edged sword. Multiple marriages marked Kyteler's life to wealthy men, including William Outlaw, Adam le Blund, Richard de Valle, and Sir John le Poer. Her husbands' untimely deaths and her subsequent inheritance of their fortunes raised suspicions among her contemporaries.

Her stepson Richard de Valle brought his accusation of witchcraft against Kyteler to Richard de Ledrede, the Bishop of Ossory. He twisted it into an elaborate Satanic conspiracy, because of his training under Pope John XXII, thereby creating a remarkable precursor of the much later European witch trials.

Being accused of witchcraft herself, Kyteler skillfully deflected blame onto others, including her maidservant, Petronilla de

Meath. Kyteler's cunning move enabled her to avoid prosecution, while her servant, Petronilla de Meath, endured brutal torture and burned at the stake. Fleeing Ireland, Kyteler escaped the troubles that plagued her life in her homeland.

Witch-hunters formally charged Kyteler with multiple accusations. Accusers charged her with denying the power of Christ and the Church, a transgression that was interpreted as worshiping the devil during this period. This was a grave offense, because people believed that renouncing one's faith could only lead to a pact with the Devil, a being of immense power and malevolence.

One accusation against Kyteler was she sacrificed animals to her supposed demon-lover, Robin, son of Artisson. Authorities said Artisson was a manifestation of pure evil. Accusations arose she offered these animals to him in exchange for dark magick and guidance in her craft. Accusations also stated that she consulted demons for witchcraft advice, a practice perceived as direct communication with the forces of darkness.

During that period, one of the most shocking allegations against Kyteler was she had a sexual relationship with the demon Robin Artisson. Said to be a demon who could take on various forms, including animals and an Ethiopian. They alleged that Robin Artisson would often appear to Kyteler in these forms, and that their relationship was a central part of her witchcraft.

They accused Kyteler of holding coven meetings and burning candles in the church at night without permission. Her accusers said a group of townsfolk attended these meetings. This included people such as Robert of Bristol, Petronilla de Midia, Petronilla's daughter Sarah, John/Ellen Syssok Galrussyn, Annota Lange, Eva de Brownstown, William Payn de Boly, and

Alice Fabri. The accusers also charged all of them with witchcraft. The authorities spread rumors that these individuals met to practice their dark magick and to further their own interests.

The accusations against Kyteler also included the creation of dark magick based powders, ointments, and potions. These were said to be made from a variety of alarming ingredients, including body parts of unbaptized children, worms, a skull, and chicken innards. Accusations arose she used these potions to corrupt and kill her husbands and to manipulate and control those around her.

Finally, they accused Kyteler of bewitching and killing her husbands to take their money for herself and her son, William Outlaw. They considered Kyteler's crime extremely heinous because they believed she used dark magick to kill her loved ones to gain wealth and power.

Her supposed transgressions were likely fueled by the societal norms of the time. But Kyteler's ability to manipulate the judicial system highlights how class and privilege could eliminate witchcraft accusations. Showing how those in positions of power, often using their influence to silence their accusers.

Kyteler's case is a testament to the complexities of the witchcraft trials, which were often characterized by a lack of concrete evidence and a reliance on hearsay and superstition. Because Kyteler was a noblewoman, she exploited her status to avoid punishment. Meanwhile, her servant, Petronilla de Meath, suffered brutal torture as the witch-hunters tried to force a confession from her. How Kyteler could deflect blame onto her servant speaks to the deep-seated prejudices of the time.

This phenomenon of accused witches becoming accusers reveals the toxic atmosphere of fear and survival. Under immense pressure, individuals acted out of desperation, manipulating the system to save themselves or gain temporary relief. This dynamic not only sustained the trials but also deepened societal divisions, pitting townsfolk and communities against one another.

Gender and class also played pivotal roles in this process. The process targeted marginalized women disproportionately, but women like Kyteler, who possessed wealth or social influence, could occasionally manipulate the system to their advantage. The reliance on coerced confessions perpetuated a cycle of fear and mistrust which helped to reinforce the patriarchal and hierarchical structures of the time.

CHAPTER II
THE WITCH-HUNTING MACHINE IN EUROPE

The European witch-hunts represent one of history's darkest chapters, spanning mostly in the 15th to 17th centuries and leaving a legacy of fear, cruelty, and mass hysteria. Throughout the continent, thousands of people, primarily women, faced accusations, trials, and execution for witchcraft. Despite shared beliefs in magick and the supernatural, local cultures, religious ideologies, and political climates influenced the intensity and methods of witch-hunting, causing them to vary widely across the continent.

Superstition and a deep-seated fear of the unknown, which was worsened by the emotional, social, and economic conditions of the time, often fueled the witch-hunts. The Black Death, which ravaged Europe in the 14th century, had left a lasting impact on the continent's demographics and economy. This led to widespread poverty, famine, and social unrest. In this climate of fear and uncertainty, people turned to scapegoating, blaming minority groups, including women, for their misfortunes.

Accusations of witchcraft frequently targeted women seen as outsiders or who displayed characteristics that were deemed suspicious. These included elderly, widowed, or childless women, as well as those perceived as healers, midwives, or practitioners of folk medicine. Neighbors, family members, or other townsfolk who were seeking to eliminate perceived threats to their social status or economic well-being often made the accusations.

The trials and executions of witches comprised a great fanfare, and both witch-hunters and torturers subjected the accused to a range of brutal and inhumane punishments. This included torture, forced confessions, and public executions by burning at the stake or hanging. A lack of due process often characterized these trials, with the accused being denied the right to a fair trial, representation, or even the opportunity to defend themselves.

The witch-hunts weren't confined to a single country or area, but spread throughout Europe, reaching many cultures and societies. The German witch-hunts were intense, with an estimated 20,000 to 30,000 people being executed for witchcraft between 1560 and 1630. In Scotland, the witch-hunts were also widespread, with about 4,000 people being executed for witchcraft between 1590 and 1662. In other countries, such as France, England, and Poland, the witch-hunts were also significant.

Germany

Germany experienced some of the largest and most brutal witch trials in European history, largely driven by religious and political tensions during the Reformation and Counter-Reformation. Among the most infamous were the Würzburg and Bamberg witch trials of the early 17th century.

The Wurzburg Witch Trials (1626-1631) are one of the largest mass-trials and mass-executions Europe had ever experienced during peacetime. The executions of hundreds of people of all ages, sexes, and classes resulted from this. Executioners burned all those found guilty at the stake, sometimes after being beheaded, sometimes while they were alive. Records confirm that executioners in Würzburg killed one hundred fifty-seven women, children, and men. An estimated 900 more people were either executed or died in custody in the prince-bishopric, an area ruled by someone with both religious and secular authority.

The first persecutions in Würzburg started with the consent of Julius Echter von Mespelbrunn, Prince bishop of Würzburg. Continuing until reaching their climax during the reign of his nephew and successor Philipp Adolf von Ehrenberg.

With the Catholic reconquest, the Catholic Church sought to reassert its authority over the regions that had been under Protestant control with the witch-trials of the 1620s. The lord or bishop of the area would be the instigator of these trials, while in others, the Jesuits played a significant role in promoting the witch-hunts. Local witch-committees sometimes formed to advance the witch-hunts, often with devastating consequences for the accused.

Among the prince-bishops, the one most active in promoting the witch-trials was Philipp Adolf von Ehrenberg of Würzburg. During his eight-year reign, he was responsible for the burning of 900 people. Von Ehrenberg also condemned his own nephew, nineteen Catholic priests, and children as young as seven to the stake, accusing them of having intercourse with demons. The sheer scale of the persecution in Würzburg was a testament to the zeal with which von Ehrenberg pursued the witch-hunts.

The witch-trials in the city began with the traditional targets of suspicion: poor working-class women. However, as the trials expanded in size and scope, the accused included men and children from all classes which were different from other witch trials. In the later years of the trials, men were sometimes the most executed. This shift in the demographics of the accused was a stark reminder of the arbitrary and unstable nature of the trials. These trials seemed to be driven more by a desire to punish and intimidate than by any genuine concern for justice.

The sheer scale of the persecution was staggering. They executed forty-three priests, which was a testament to the fact that no one was above suspicion. Ernst von Ehrenberg, the nephew of the Prince Bishop himself, was among the victims. This became a tragic reminder that even the highest echelons of society were not immune to the madness that gripped the city. Authorities confirmed the execution of at least 49 children under the age of twelve, many of whom came from the orphanage and school Julius-Spital. The city, being entrusted with their care, brutally and inhumanely murdered these children, cutting their lives short in a frenzy of fear and superstition.

A contemporary letter from 1629 paints a vivid picture of the chaos and terror that gripped the city. According to the letter, people of all ages and classes were being arrested every day. The witch-hunters accused them of attending the witches' sabbat and being noted in the black book of Satan. Interestingly enough, they searched for this book but were never able to locate it. Authorities accused a third of the population of being in league with the Devil, a staggering figure that underscores the sheer scale of the persecution. People from all walks of life were being arrested and charged, regardless of age, profession, or sex, for reasons ranging from murder and satanism to the most trivial of offenses.

Authorities even accused some people of humming a song mentioning the Devil, while arresting others for vagrancy because they could not satisfactorily explain their business in town. Records show a total of 32 people appear to have been vagrants. A shocking reminder that even the most vulnerable members of society were not immune to the cruelty and injustice of the trials.

The Bamberg Witch Trials took place in the early 17th century (1626-1631) and were a series of mass executions that occurred in the small state of Bamberg. The Prince-Bishop Gottfried Johann Georg II Fuchs von Dornheim ruled this region. Widespread devastation marked this period, being ravaged by years of war and conflicts within the Holy Roman Empire, as well as a series of crop failures, famines, and plagues. The people of Bamberg, desperate for answers and seeking a scapegoat for their troubles, turned to the supernatural, and accusations of witchcraft increased rapidly.

Taking advantage of this atmosphere of fear and superstition, Fuchs von Dornheim oversaw the establishment of a network of informers. Fuchs von Dornheim tasked them with gathering information and making accusations against suspected witches. He ensured these accusations remained secret, and he refused to grant the accused any legal rights, preventing them from defending themselves. Fuchs von Dornheim also established an operation of full-time torturers and executioners, who subjected the accused to brutal and inhumane treatment.

They built the notorious Drudenhaus, or witch prison, in Bamberg in 1627 to house the special torture chambers. This prison was a place of unspeakable horror, where they subjected the accused to thumbscrews and vises, ice-cold baths and scalding lime baths. The guards whipped the accused, burned them with sulphur, put them in iron-spiked stocks, and subjected them to other forms of torture. Often leaving the victims to suffer for days, even weeks, before being executed. Torturers killed children as young as 6 years old. Sometimes, even after sentencing the accused, they continued to physically abuse them, cutting off their hands as they led them to the stake.

Many rich and powerful people of the area fell victim to the frenzy of accusations and had their property and assets confiscated, which made Dornheim and his officers extremely rich. Dornheim and his officers arrested anyone who questioned what was happening and subjected them to the same treatment. The atmosphere of fear and paranoia was everywhere, and it appeared no one was safe from the accusations of witchcraft.

Johannes Junius was the bürgermeister (mayor) of Bamberg, who became a victim of the Bamberg Witch Trials. In 1628, they accused Junius of witchcraft because they had executed his wife for witchcraft. Georg Neudecker, another bürgermeister, also accused Junius of witchcraft following his own imprisonment and implicated Junius as an accomplice. Other suspected witches also implicated Junius in their confessions.

Records describe how Junius at first denied all charges and demanded to confront his witnesses and continued to deny his involvement in witchcraft. After weeks of torture, which included the application of thumbscrews, leg vises, and the strappado, he finally confessed on July 5, 1628. He claimed he had renounced God for the Devil, and he had seen twenty-seven of his colleagues at a Sabbat.

In his confession, Junius recounts a dark period in his life where he was financially struggling. A woman who turned out to be a malevolent spirit deceived him, forcing him to renounce his faith in God. After being attacked by demons, Junius eventually surrendered and accepted the Devil as his deity, adopting the witch-name Krix and receiving a familiar named Füchsin. Junius soon learned that several locals also worshipped Satan and took part in the witches' sabbats, often riding a monstrous black dog.

At one of these gatherings, Junius said he went to a Black Mass where Beelzebub appeared. Beelzebub then commanded Junius to kill his children, but he punished Junius for his refusal to do it. However, he admitted to sacrificing his horse and burying a sacred wafer. In his last letter to his daughter, he claimed he confessed under duress and was innocent. One month later, they publicly burned Junius to death.

It took complaints from several influential people to get Emperor Ferdinand to issue mandates against the persecution in 1630 and 1631. However, by this time, the damage had already been done, and the Bamberg Witch Trials had left a lasting scar on the community.

Figures like Balthasar von Dernbach and Nicholas Remy played a pivotal role in laying the groundwork for these witch trials. They did so by promoting the use of torture and advocating for the eradication of witches as a societal plague.

In other regions, the persecution was equally brutal. In Baden, recently reconquered for Catholicism by Tilly, the years 1627-1629 were dreadful. In the Ortenau region, authorities executed 70 people, while in Offenburg, they burned 79 victims at the stake. A judge in Eichstätt, a Bavarian prince-bishopric, reported killing 274 witches in 1629, although the accuracy of this figure is difficult to verify.

Executioners killed 50 people in Reichertshofen, in the district of Neuburg an der Donau, between November 1628 and August 1630. However, the persecution extended beyond these specific regions. The three prince-archbishoprics of the Rhineland also experienced the devastating effects of these fires. At Coblenz, the seat of the prince-archbishop of Trier, burnt 24 witches in 1629, while at Sélestat, they executed at least 30 people, at the beginning of a five-year persecution.

In Mainz, the burnings continued as well, with the local authorities seemingly unable to stop the witch-hunts. At Cologne, the City Fathers had always been merciful, much to the annoyance of the prince-archbishop, who had long sought to impose his will on the city. However, in 1627, he put pressure on the city, and it eventually gave in to his demands. Naturally enough, the persecution raged most violently in Bonn, the prince-archbishop's own capital. In Bonn, the prince-archbishop executed the chancellor and his wife, the archbishop's secretary's wife. Accusers even branded children as young as three and four years old for having devils as their lovers. And they even sent students and small boys of noble birth to the bonfire.

Scotland

Witch trials in Scotland reached their peak during the reign of King James VI, a monarch deeply interested in witchcraft and its supposed threats. His book, *Daemonologie*, provided a theological and legal framework for prosecuting witches, which helped to fuel a nationwide witch-hunting frenzy. The book was a comprehensive guide to the detection and prosecution of witches. It drew on a range of sources, including biblical scripture, medieval folklore, and contemporary accounts of witch trials. The book argued that witchcraft was a mortal sin deserving of death.

One of the earliest Scottish witch trials occurred in North Berwick (1590-1592), a small town on the east coast of Scotland. The trials resulted from a string of events hinting at a plot to conjure storms and wreck the king's ship sailing from Denmark. A group of local women, many of whom were elderly and poor, faced accusations of witchcraft and conspiring with the devil to bring about the king's downfall. The trials were marked by a series of gruesome and coercive methods, including torture, which were used to extract confessions from the accused.

The trials in North Berwick were a prime example of the methods used to detect and prosecute witches during this period. Torturers subjected accused witches to a range of physical and psychological torments. This included stretching them on the rack, breaking their fingers and toes, and forcing them to confess to pacts with the Devil while taking part in sabbats. Authorities widely used and accepted torture as a legitimate way to extract confessions, and they coerced many of the accused into making false confessions to avoid further suffering. The trials also featured public executions, with many of the accused being burned at the stake, a spectacle reinforcing fear and legitimizing future trials.

The North Berwick Witch Trials were a significant event in Scottish history, marking the beginning of a period of intense witch-hunting that would last for several decades. Being widely publicized, the trials helped to create a climate of fear and hysteria. Authorities took the accusations of witchcraft seriously, and they often subjected the accused to brutal and inhumane punishments.

We've already read the atrocities of witch-hunters like Pierre de Lancre and Sebastian Michaelis in previous chapters. But we must again mention their notable witch-hunting campaigns in 17th-century France because of the sheer brutality. They too used mass accusations and public executions along with torture to extract confessions blending theological discourse with sensational accounts of witchcraft.

The European witch-hunts were far from uniform, shaped by regional differences in culture, religion, and governance. This diversity of approaches and attitudes towards witchcraft is a testament to the complex and multifaceted nature of the witch-hunting phenomenon. Figures like Balthasar von Dernbach, Nicholas Remy, King James VI, Pierre de Lancre, and Sebastian Michaelis played pivotal roles in shaping the character of these trials. Whether through their zealous advocacy for persecution or their development of distinct methods.

Von Dernbach's advocacy for the use of torture to extract confessions, for example, was a hallmark of the German witch-hunts, while Remy's writings on witchcraft helped to fuel the witch-hunting frenzy in France. King James VI's book, *Daemonologie*, provided a theological and legal framework for prosecuting witches in Scotland. While mass accusations and public executions marked de Lancre's witch-hunting campaign in the Basque region. Michaelis' inquisitorial cases, meanwhile, reflected the growing influence of the Counter-Reformation, which sought to eradicate perceived threats to Catholic orthodoxy through aggressive witch-hunting.

CHAPTER 12
WITCH-HUNTING IN ENGLAND AND SCOTLAND

The English and Scottish witch trials remain among the most infamous episodes in the history of European witch-hunting, a period marked by widespread fear, superstition, and violence. Spanning from the mid-16th century to the late 17th century. A complex interplay of factors fueled these trials, including religious upheaval, legal reforms, and social tensions that had been simmering for centuries.

England's tumultuous history with Catholicism, outlawed since Henry VIII, largely fueled its witch trials. The English Reformation had created a power vacuum, with the Church of England emerging as a compromise between Catholicism and Protestantism. The power vacuum fostered a climate of suspicion and mistrust, especially toward women viewed as potential agents of the Devil. The country's unique legal system, which relied heavily on common law and the testimony of witnesses, also influenced the English witch trials.

In contrast, its distinct cultural and religious heritage shaped Scotland's approach to prosecuting witchcraft. The country's powerful tradition of folk magick and the supernatural, combined with its adherence to Presbyterianism, created a unique cultural landscape in which witchcraft was a serious threat to the community. A more formalized and bureaucratic approach also characterized the Scottish witch trials, with the establishment of the Scottish Privy Council's Commission on Witchcraft in 1590.

Despite these differences, both England and Scotland shared a common thread in their approach to witchcraft: the use of torture and coercion to extract confessions from accused witches. The brutal and ineffective "swimming test," a method of determining guilt, involved throwing accused witches into water to see if they would sink or float. Using such methods led to the execution of thousands of people, most of whom were women, on charges of witchcraft.

The 1563 Witchcraft Act significantly shaped the English witch trials under Elizabeth I, which made witchcraft a capital offense if it resulted in harm or death. Later, the 1604 Act under James I expanded the definition of witchcraft to include dealings with "evil spirits," increasing the intensity of witch-hunting.

Unlike continental Europe, England did not officially sanction torture. However, officials often used informal methods of coercion. Witch trials frequently relied on witness testimony, particularly that of neighbors and sometimes children.

The 1563 Scottish Witchcraft Act mirrored the English Act, but Scotland enforced it more ferociously. King James VI's personal interest in witchcraft, as shown in his treatise, *Daemonologie*, intensified the witch-hunting fervor. Scottish trials often involved brutal methods of torture, including pricking for "witch-marks" and the use of the "witch's bridle".

The Scottish legal system permitted torture under the authorization of the Privy Council, leading to widespread confessions extracted under duress. Trials in Scotland often resulted in execution by burning, reflecting a deeply entrenched belief in the danger posed by witches.

James VI's *Daemonologie* helped to shape witch-hunting practices in both England and Scotland. His obsession with witchcraft stemmed from personal experiences, including the North Berwick trials, which he believed were part of a conspiracy to assassinate him.

As King of England, James continued to support witch-hunting, influencing the drafting of the 1604 Witchcraft Act. His reign saw an increase in prosecutions, particularly in cases involving alleged pacts with the Devil.

As we know from a previous chapter, Roger Nowell, a magistrate in Lancashire, presided over the famous Pendle Witch Trials of 1612. Nowell's investigations led to one of the most notorious cases in English history, highlighting the role of local officials in instigating witch-hunting.

In August 1612, a series of trials took place in Lancaster, England, known as the Lancashire Witch Trials. Among these trials were the Pendle Witch Trials, which involved 12 accused witches from the area surrounding Pendle Hill in Lancashire. The trials were notable for their documentation and the number of executions that followed.

The trials of the accused witches took place at Lancaster Assizes on August 18-19, 1612, amidst a climate of fear and superstition. Because of the severity of her alleged crimes, they tried Jennet Preston separately at York Assizes on July 27, 1612. Unfortunately, another accused, Elizabeth Southerns, died in prison before her trial, likely because of the harsh conditions and lack of proper medical care.

The verdicts of the 11 individuals who went to trial were overwhelmingly in favor of the prosecution. The court hanged ten of the accused after finding them guilty; this gruesome and public spectacle served as a warning to others suspected of witchcraft. Only Alice Gray received a not-guilty verdict. This is a rare instance of justice being served in a system that often prioritized fear and retribution over fairness and due process.

Some of the accused witches confessed to their crimes, providing disturbing details about their alleged activities. Alizon Device, for example, claimed to have sold her soul to the Devil and to have caused a stroke in a peddler named John Law, demonstrating the twisted and fantastical nature of her confessions. Elizabeth Device and Anne Whittle also confessed, describing their alleged witchcraft activities and accusing others of similar crimes. These confessions, while likely coerced, added to the sense of hysteria and paranoia that characterized the trials and served as a testament.

The Pendle Witch Trials stand as one of the most infamous and well-documented witch trials in English history, possessing a rich and complex legacy that continues to captivate historians and the public alike. These trials have been the subject of many books, plays, and films, each offering a unique perspective on this dark and fascinating chapter in the country's past. The trials themselves were a pivotal moment in the history of witchcraft in England, and their significance extended far beyond the small village of Pendle in Lancashire.

One of the most remarkable aspects of the Pendle Witch Trials is that Thomas Potts, the court clerk, documented them in an official publication, *The Wonderfull Discoverie of Witches in the*

Countie of Lancaster. This detailed account provides a unique insight into the trials, allowing modern-day readers to experience the drama and intrigue of the proceedings firsthand. The publication is a testament to the meticulous record-keeping of the time, and its existence has enabled historians to reconstruct the events of the trials with remarkable accuracy.

Accusers charged the Pendle witches with a range of alleged crimes, including murder, bewitchment, and cursing, and claimed they used their supposed powers to harm livestock and humans alike. The accusations were often based on hearsay and rumor, and a lack of due process and a reliance on dubious evidence marked the trials themselves. Despite these flaws, the trials had a profound impact on the lives of those involved, and their legacy continues to be felt to this day.

As we have previously read, the Essex Witch Trials were a dark and disturbing chapter in the history of English witch-hunting. They were part of a broader wave of prosecutions that swept the country during the tumultuous English Civil War. Conducted under the guidance of the notorious witch-finder, Matthew Hopkins and his associate John Stearne. These trials resulted in numerous executions, often based on coerced confessions extracted through the use of torture and intimidation. The Essex trials were among the most extensive in England, with hundreds of people accused of witchcraft and subjected to a range of dubious and often brutal tests designed to prove their guilt.

One of the most infamous features of the Essex trials was the use of the "swimming tests", a method of determining guilt that was both cruel and ineffective. They threw suspects into the water, deeming them guilty of witchcraft if they floated. This test was based on the superstition that witches could not sink in water because of their supposed pact with the Devil. Torture and coercion often preceded the test, allowing investigators to extract confessions from the weakened suspects. They subjected those who floated to further torture and interrogation. Investigators sometimes left those who sank to drown.

The Essex trials also reflected the widespread fear and social instability of the Civil War period. The conflict had created a climate of anxiety and mistrust, with many people seeking scapegoats for the troubles that had befallen the country. Accusations of witchcraft frequently blamed the Devil or other external forces for the era's problems, avoiding the underlying social and economic issues. Trials frequently targeted women viewed as outsiders or practitioners of folk magick, particularly in rural areas.

Hopkins and Stearne, the masterminds behind the Essex trials, operated outside the formal judicial system, exploiting local fears to justify their actions. They used a range of tactics, including the use of informants and the dissemination of propaganda, to create a climate of fear and hysteria. They also developed a range of dubious tests and techniques, including the use of "touching tests" to determine whether a suspect had made a pact with the Devil. These tests were often based on superstition and folklore, rather than any scientific or rational evidence.

The North Berwick Witch Trials were a series of witchcraft persecutions that took place in East Lothian, Scotland, between 1590 and 1592. A series of storms that disrupted King James VI's voyage back to Scotland from Denmark sparked these trials. The king's journey to Denmark in 1589 was a significant event, marking the beginning of a new era in the royal family. King James VI had traveled to Denmark to marry Anne of Denmark, a union that would strengthen the ties between Scotland and Denmark.

During the return journey, his ship encountered severe storms that threatened the safety of the royal party. The storms were so intense that they forced the king's ship to seek shelter in the port of North Berwick, a small town in East Lothian. The Danish admiral, Peder Munk, who was on board the ship, attributed the storms to witchcraft. This led to a witch-hunt in Denmark, resulting in the execution of several women accused of causing the storms. The accusations were likely fueled by superstition and a desire to blame the unpredictable weather on a perceived enemy.

In Scotland, King James VI became convinced that witches from North Berwick were responsible for the storms that had beset his voyage. The witch trials that followed directly resulted from the king's experience in Denmark. A series of accusations, confessions, and executions characterized the trials. Accusations of witchcraft targeted many women, and some confessed to crimes they did not commit. A lack of due process and a reliance on dubious evidence, such as "spectral evidence", testimony about dreams and visions, marked the trials. The trials ultimately led to the execution of several women, whom they burned at the stake or hanged for their alleged crimes.

The North Berwick Witch Trials are one of the most infamous witch-hunts in Scottish history, a dark chapter that left a lasting impact on the country's judicial system and the lives of its people. The trials led to the execution of over 70 people, mostly women, accused of witchcraft and subsequently burned at the stake or hanged. This wave of persecution marked a turning point in King James VI's views on witchcraft, which had previously been more nuanced and open-minded.

Prior to the North Berwick Witch Trials, King James VI had shown a more measured approach to witchcraft, recognizing that many accusations were based on superstition and fear. However, the trials in Scotland, which were sparked by his own experiences in Denmark, seemed to galvanize his views on the subject. His treatise, *Daemonologie*, solidified his belief in the existence of witchcraft and the need for severe punishment. In this influential work, the king outlined his views on witchcraft; the methods used by witches to cast spells, and the importance of rooting out this perceived evil from society.

As the 17th century drew to a close, a growing sense of skepticism permeated the air, casting a shadow over the witch-hunting fervor that had gripped Europe for centuries. In England, the tide of public opinion was slowly turning against the witch trials, as people began to question the validity of the accusations, and the dubious methods used to extract confessions. A growing awareness of these flaws fueled a shift in attitude in the witch-hunting process. Including the use of coerced confessions, dubious tests, and the targeting of vulnerable individuals, particularly women.

The 1735 Witchcraft Act, passed during the reign of King George II, marked a significant turning point in the history of witch-hunting in England. This landmark legislation effectively brought an end to the witch trials, redefining witchcraft as a form of fraudulent behavior rather than a supernatural crime. The Act clarified that witchcraft was no longer a legitimate reason for prosecution and instead treated it as a form of deception or charlatanism. This shift in the law reflected a growing recognition of the need for due process and protecting individual rights, as well as a more rational and scientific approach to understanding the world.

In Scotland, the last execution for witchcraft occurred in 1727, marking the end of a long and bloody chapter in the country's history. Parliament repealed the 1563 Witchcraft Act in 1736, effectively ending the witch trials in Scotland. This development was a testament to the growing influence of Enlightenment thinking, which emphasized reason, science, and protecting individual rights. As the 18th century dawned, Scotland and England were both moving away from the superstition and fear that had driven the witch-hunting frenzy towards a more rational and enlightened approach to understanding the world.

The decline of witch-hunting in England and Scotland was a gradual process, marked by a series of small but significant steps towards greater skepticism and rationality. As the 18th century progressed, the idea of witchcraft as a supernatural force faded, replaced by a more nuanced understanding of the social and cultural factors that had driven the witch-hunting frenzy. The witch trials' legacy continued to shape the lives of its victims, but the era of mass hysteria and persecution finally ended.

CHAPTER 13
FEAR AND HYSTERIA IN COLONIAL AMERICA

Few events in early American history evoke as much fascination, horror, and reflection as the Salem Witch Trials. Taking place between February 1692 and May 1693, these trials left an indelible mark on colonial America. They continue to this day to be a cautionary tale of the dangers of mass hysteria and injustice. In the tightly knit and deeply religious Puritan community of Salem, Massachusetts. A place where suspicion and fear collided with deeply rooted social tensions. This led to one of the most infamous witch-hunts in history.

To understand the Salem Witch Trials, one must first appreciate the Puritan worldview that shaped the colony's social and religious fabric. The Puritans, who had fled religious persecution in England, established communities in New England, based on strict adherence to their interpretation of the Bible. Their theology emphasized the constant battle between good and evil, with God's chosen people on one side and Satan and his followers on the other. Any deviation from Puritan orthodoxy was a potential opening for the Devil's influence.

In this context, they considered witchcraft a direct alliance with Satan, and Puritans believed witches sought to harm others through supernatural means. The fear of witchcraft was not unique to New England. Europe had already witnessed centuries of witch-hunts, but in Salem, the community's isolation and deep anxieties exacerbated the paranoia of their survival.

By the late 17th century, Salem Village, a rural farming community, now Danvers, Massachusetts, and nearby Salem Town, a bustling port, were rife with economic and social divisions. Salem Village, in particular, was struggling. Crop failures, Native American raids on frontier settlements, and disputes over land ownership added to the villagers' stress. There were also bitter disagreements over the appointment of Reverend Samuel Parris, whose fiery sermons often stoked the fear of divine wrath and demonic forces.

These divisions fractured the community, creating factions that distrusted one another. Within this climate of suspicion, accusations of witchcraft offered an outlet for simmering resentments and a means of targeting those who deviated from societal norms.

It all began in early 1692 when several young girls in Salem Village began exhibiting bizarre symptoms. Nine-year-old Betty Parris and her cousin, eleven-year-old Abigail Williams, were the first to suffer from fits, screaming uncontrollably, contorting their bodies, and claiming to see visions of spectral creatures. Soon, other girls in the village, including Ann Putnam Jr. and Mary Walcott, displayed similar behaviors.

When doctors could find no physical explanation, the community turned to the supernatural. Pressured to name the source of their torment, the girls accused three women: Tituba, Sarah

Good, and Sarah Osborne. These three women were easy targets because of their marginalized social standing.

Tituba played the most pivotal role in igniting the hysteria. Though interrogated last, she confessed to practicing witchcraft under weeks of duress and claimed that someone had coerced her and others in the village into serving the Devil. Samuel Parris, the minister whose household was the supposed origin of the witchcraft, held Tituba in slavery. Although authorities officially charged her with witchcraft against four Salem girls between January and March, there are no court records that precisely say why someone accused Tituba. She was especially close to 9-year-old Betty Parris. She had worked and prayed alongside the family for years, for at least a decade in Boston and Salem.

Her testimony was vivid and fantastical, describing visions of black dogs, mysterious birds, and a man in a black coat who demanded her allegiance. Her confession lent credibility to the accusations and spurred further investigations.

Sarah Good was a homeless beggar, and Sarah Osborne was an elderly widow with a tarnished reputation. They were among the first to be accused of witchcraft in the Salem Witch Trials. Their marginalized positions in society made them easy targets for the accusations, as the townsfolk already viewed them with suspicion and disdain. Sarah Good, with her tattered clothing and constant begging, was a nuisance, a reminder of the darker aspects of society that many preferred to ignore. Sarah Osborne, on the other hand, was a widow with a reputation for being eccentric and possibly even unorthodox in her views. Her advanced age and perceived independence made her a convenient target for those seeking to settle old scores or eliminate perceived threats to their social status.

As vulnerable members of society, Good and Osborne were susceptible to the accusations of witchcraft. Their lack of social standing and economic security made them powerless to defend themselves against the charges. Their living circumstances had already tarnished their reputations. The accusations against them were a combination of prejudice, fear, and misinformation, fueled by the hysteria and paranoia that gripped the community. The accusation of them alongside Tituba, the enslaved woman to the Parris household, further fueled the chaos and confusion, as reality and fantasy increasingly blurred.

As the Salem Witch Trials continued to unfold, the accusations targeted even the most respected members of the community. Rebecca Nurse, a revered elderly woman in her late 60s, was among those accused, despite her impeccable reputation and decades of devoted service to the community. Her spotless character and unwavering commitment to her faith made her a pillar of the community, and her accusation sent shockwaves through the village. The court leveled baseless charges against her, lacking any credible evidence. Yet they subjected her to the same brutal treatment as the others, forcing her to endure the humiliation of a chained public parade and the court's whims.

Giles Corey, a farmer in his 80s, was another prominent figure who refused to be intimidated by the accusations. Although he was one of the oldest and most respected members of the community, they accused him of witchcraft and subjected him to the same cruel treatment as the others. When asked to plead guilty, Corey famously refused, stating "more weight" would be required to extract a confession from him. His defiance in the face of overwhelming pressure was a testament to his unwavering commitment to his innocence. Authorities saw his refusal to cooperate with the court as a threat to the very fabric of the justice system. The court brutally used violence to extract confessions, pressing Corey to death with heavy stones. They intended this punishment to break his spirit and force his cooperation. The cases of Rebecca Nurse and Giles Corey starkly revealed the accusations' arbitrariness and cruelty, and the dangers of a justice system that prioritized confession over evidence.

The Salem Witch Trials are notorious for their reliance on "spectral evidence," the form of testimony where witnesses claim to see the specter of the accused committing acts of witchcraft. The specter would typically come in the form of a spirit or a ghostly figure. Puritans believed the Devil couldn't impersonate the innocent, making the accused's spectral appearance in a victim's vision irrefutable evidence.

This type of evidence was highly subjective and impossible to verify, yet it became the cornerstone of many convictions. The afflicted girls often gave dramatic testimony, claiming they were physically attacked by the invisible specters of the accused during court sessions. The afflicted girls' accusations frequently prompted theatrical fainting, screaming, and writhing, further convincing judges and spectators of the accused's guilt.

Although not historically accurate and based mainly on popular culture, we must mention Cotton Mather. Today, popular culture portrays him as one of the main witch-hunters. However, history shows us he was not even involved in the trial proceedings. Before the outbreak of accusations in Salem Village, Mather had already published his account, Remarkable Providences (1684), describing the possession of the children of the Goodwin family of Boston. However, this has a tremendous influence on the courts during that time.

Mather's publication of *The Wonders of the Invisible World* in October 1692, after the last executions, perhaps makes up one of the main reasons many consider him involved. This publication served as a testament to the fervor and conviction of the Salem Witch Trials. In it, his words described, and somewhat justified, the trials and deaths that had taken place that year. However, the book is anything but resolved regarding Mather's true feelings about the trials, leaving readers to question his sincerity and motives.

Although he insisted, he wrote the book without malice or prejudice and only wrote from the records of the trials, his words paint a starkly different picture. He writes of the trials of accused witches such as Bridget Bishop, saying there was "little occasion to prove witchcraft, it being clear and notorious to all beholders." This statement is striking, as it highlights the lack of due process and the reliance on flimsy evidence that characterized the trials. His description of Susanna Martin as "one of the most impudent, scurrilous, wicked creatures in the world" is a scathing indictment of the accused. This contradictory statement served to further demonize her in the eyes of the public.

Perhaps most confusing of all, however, is Mather's condoning the use of spectral evidence to convict the witches in five cases outlined in the book. Modern standards widely regarded this type of evidence, based on testimony from afflicted individuals claiming to see visions or specters of the accused, as unreliable and perhaps even laughable. Yet Cotton saw fit to include it as evidence, further perpetuating the hysteria and fear that had gripped the community.

In Mather's letter to William Stoughton, penned during the trial of George Burroughs, he also asserts the guilt of this man.

In it, he stated Burroughs was the ringleader of 10 other witches. This claim is based on a confession received from five Andover witches, which Cotton describes as "refreshing his soul." This statement is particularly telling, as it highlights Cotton's willingness to accept dubious evidence and his own biases in order to further the cause of the trials.

Although Mather was not directly involved in the proceedings of the Salem Witch Trials, he penned a contradictory letter to John Richards, a prominent magistrate in Boston. Where he cautioned against the use of spectral evidence. This letter is possibly a testament to Mather's growing unease with the trials. Or perhaps served as a subtle yet significant attempt to rein in the fervor that had gripped the community.

Besides this letter, Mather also wrote the *Return of the Several Ministers*, a carefully crafted report sent to the judges of the Salem court. This document is a masterful exercise in diplomatic language and advised caution in using spectral evidence. Though he acknowledged the Devil was cunning enough to assume the shape of an innocent person. In the same document, Mather's decries the use of spectral evidence, describing it as "noise, company, and openness." He also criticized the reliance on witch-tests such as the recitation of the Lord's Prayer. However, the last paragraph of the document appears to undermine this cautionary statement, recommending the "detection of witchcrafts" in a manner that seems to legitimize the trials.

In the opinions of scholars Bernard Rosenthal and Perry Miller, the courts interpreted Mather's letter and report as a seal of approval for the trials to continue. This reading is not entirely unfounded, as the language of the report, while cautious, seems to suggest a begrudging acceptance of the trials' legitimacy.

Ultimately, the momentum of the trials overshadowed Mather's efforts, if any, to rein in the hysteria, leaving his true intentions and motivations open to interpretation.

The establishment of the special Court of Oyer and Terminer in 1692 to handle witchcraft cases exacerbated the hysteria. Presided over by judges such as William Stoughton and Samuel Sewall, the court operated under the assumption that witchcraft was real and present in Salem. They prioritized extracting confessions, often through aggressive interrogations or threats of execution. To avoid execution, confessors often named other alleged witches, thus continuing the cycle of accusations.

Beyond spectral evidence, judges also used physical signs such as "witch-marks" as proof. Investigators conducted "touch-tests," asking the accused to touch their supposed victims to see if it eased their symptoms. The result was a witch-hunt of unprecedented ferocity. One that would ultimately claim the lives of dozens of innocent people and leave a lasting stain on the history of colonial America.

By the fall of 1692, the hysteria surrounding the Salem Witch Trials subsided, but not before altering a staggering number of lives forever. Records show over 200 people, mostly women, faced accusations of witchcraft, and many more faced suspicion and intimidation. We don't know the exact number of those accused. However, authorities hanged 14 women and 5 men, and they pressed one man to death. This historical count does not include the 5 who died while awaiting trial.

The reign of terror that had gripped Salem and the surrounding communities had subsided by late September, though its impact would be felt for centuries to come. A toxic mix of fear, superstition, and politics fueled the trials, leaving deep scars on the community. The legacy of the witch trials will endure as a cautionary tale about the dangers of unchecked power and the importance of upholding due process.

Finally, after the dust settled, the people of Salem and the surrounding areas began the long process of rebuilding and healing. The release of many of those accused and imprisoned eventually followed, although some would never fully recover from their ordeal. Among those was one of the first three accused of witchcraft, Tituba. The first to confess to a diabolical pact, she was ultimately the last suspect released from prison. Authorities subjected Tituba to their cruel whims for 15 harrowing months, making her endure the unbearable weight of suspicion and fear. But when she finally went on trial on May 9, 1693, the jury saw through the hysteria and declined to indict her.

This was no insignificant victory, for Tituba had been the first to break under the pressure of interrogation, naming her supposed accomplices in a desperate bid for mercy. But in the end, it was her own words that proved her salvation, as the jury recognized the coerced nature of her confession. And so, she was finally free to leave the prison that had held her captive for so long.

But Tituba's release was not just a personal triumph, it was also a powerful rebuke to the very system that had sought to destroy her. The Parris family, who had been instrumental in her downfall, could never command the same level of attention and deference over her. She appears to have left Massachusetts with whoever paid her jail fees. And as for Tituba herself, she escaped the clutches of her tormentors, disappearing from the record but living to tell the tale of her ordeal. It's a powerful reminder that even in the darkest of times, truth and justice can ultimately prevail.

The trials had exposed deep-seated fears and prejudices, and it would take time for the community to come to terms with what had happened. Even after the passage of time, the memory of the Salem Witch Trials still draws our attention and awe.

In January 1697, the Massachusetts General Court declared a day of fasting for the tragedy of the Salem Witch Trials. The same court later deemed the trials unlawful, and the leading justice Samuel Sewall publicly apologized for his role in the process. The damage to the community lingered, however, even after Massachusetts Colony passed legislation restoring the good names of the condemned and providing financial restitution to their heirs in 1711.

CHAPTER 14
WITCH-HUNTS BEYOND EUROPE AND THE NEW WORLD

Europe and North America are often associated with the most infamous witch trials. Such as the Salem Witch Trials in colonial America and the mass executions during the European witch craze of the 16th and 17th centuries. However, witch-hunts are far from being purely a Western phenomenon. Across the globe, societies in Africa, Asia, Latin America, and other regions have long grappled with their own distinct forms of witchcraft accusations and persecution. Unique cultural, social, political, and spiritual contexts that vary significantly across regions deeply influenced these practices, while sometimes sharing common themes like scapegoating or fear of the supernatural.

Some cultures still view witchcraft not as a pact with evil, but as a practical, malevolent power individuals wield to harm others. This distinction shapes how people perceive and punish witchcraft. For instance, the religious orthodoxy and fears of heresy often tied the European witch trials together. But the witch-hunts in many African and Asian societies are more closely linked to localized spiritual beliefs, familial disputes, or economic anxieties. In these contexts, people often explain misfortunes, illness, infertility, natural disasters, or unexplained deaths as malevolent supernatural interference, considering it witchcraft.

Beyond these spiritual and cultural dimensions, witch-hunts frequently intersect with broader societal pressures. Political instability, economic hardship, and social inequality often increase tensions, making communities more prone to accusing vulnerable individuals. Like Europe and colonial America, it is the women, children, or the elderly which are most often accused of witchcraft. Sometimes, accusations of witchcraft serve as a tool for consolidating power, settling personal vendettas, or redistributing resources, such as land or property. The interplay between these factors illustrates how witch-hunts are not just isolated superstitious events, but reflections of the underlying stresses and fractures within any society.

These witch-hunts are not a phenomenon of the distant past. While European and North American witch trials ended centuries ago, witchcraft accusations and persecutions remain a reality in many parts of the world. From the "witch-camps" of Ghana to the persecution of "child-witches" in parts of Nigeria and Congo. To this day, there are practices in regions of India, Papua New Guinea, and Latin America where the belief and fear of witchcraft continue with violence, exile, and societal division. These contemporary witch-hunts often exist in regions where traditional beliefs coexist uneasily with modern legal systems. This creates a complex environment in which both ancient practices and contemporary challenges contribute to the persistence of witchcraft-related violence.

Africa

In many parts of Africa, the belief in witchcraft is deeply ingrained in the cultural and spiritual fabric of society. Various terms, such as "juju", "muti", or "nganga", identify witchcraft, which people often view as a potent and malevolent force used to harm others. The European views on witchcraft often emphasized diabolical pacts with Satan or heretical behavior. African perceptions of witchcraft are more grounded in the idea of interpersonal harm as an unseen power that operates within families, villages, and communities.

People often link this complex and multifaceted concept of witchcraft to a person's spiritual or mystical powers, which are used for both good and evil. In some African cultures, people believe witches possess a unique spiritual energy harnessed for beneficial or malevolent purposes. A person's ancestry, social status, and personal relationships often closely tie this energy, believing it to be a powerful tool to influence others' lives.

Witchcraft frequently serves as a convenient explanation for personal and communal struggles, as people attribute misfortunes such as illness, infertility, sudden deaths, crop failures, and economic hardship to it. Many times, a person's envy, jealousy, or resentment causes these misfortunes towards others, which can manifest as a form of spiritual attack. This can lead to a cycle of fear, suspicion, and mistrust, as individuals become increasingly paranoid about being targeted by witches.

This widespread belief in witchcraft has severe consequences, particularly for those accused of practicing it. Accusations of witchcraft sometimes result in physical punishment, ostracism, or even death for individuals. This has led to a culture of fear and intimidation, where villagers are reluctant to speak out against accusations of witchcraft. As a result, many individuals live in constant fear of being accused, and the stigma surrounding witchcraft can have a profound impact on a person's mental and emotional well-being.

One of the key figures in this spiritual landscape is the healer or diviner, often referred to as a "witch doctor", "traditional healer", or "shaman." These individuals are the agents between the spiritual and physical worlds. People believe in their ability to diagnose supernatural causes of misfortune. They offer remedies or rituals to neutralize the effects of witchcraft. Their knowledge and expertise often earn them respect. However, these figures can also reinforce the fear of witches by identifying supposed perpetrators, which can lead to further accusations and violence.

Witchcraft accusations often arise within close-knit communities or extended families, where tensions and grievances can simmer just below the surface. For example, jealousy, disputes over inheritance, or resentment over perceived favoritism can all contribute to accusations of witchcraft. In these situations, the accusation of witchcraft can be used to enforce social norms and punishing those who deviate from expected behaviors. People may target individuals viewed as outsiders, nonconformists, or even the overly successful, suspecting them of using their supposed powers to harm others.

Besides the social control aspect, witchcraft accusations can also serve to scapegoat individuals or groups considered threats to the community. This can be particularly true in situations where there are underlying tensions or conflicts between different groups or villages. By accusing someone of witchcraft, a community can deflect attention away from its own problems and onto the supposed perpetrator, often with devastating consequences for the accused individual.

Witchcraft accusations frequently lead to severe consequences, ranging from banishment to violence and even death. The following examples highlight the scale and persistence of ongoing witch-hunts in African societies.

Tanzania has one of the highest rates of witch-related violence in Africa, with older women being vulnerable. Accusations of witchcraft frequently target widows and elderly women, particularly those with red eyes. The red eyes come from a medical condition linked to smoke exposure from cooking fires, but many interpreted this as a sign of sorcery.

These accusations are often driven by underlying economic factors, such as disputes over land or inheritance. Once labeled as witches, these women may face violent attacks, including beatings or murder, known as "witch-killings."

In Ghana, authorities often exile accused witches to "witch-camps," isolated settlements where they live in poor conditions, separated from their families and villages. These camps are designed to protect the accused from mob violence, but they also perpetuate their marginalization. Most of the residents are older women, whom many of their own relatives or neighbors accused them. Once exiled to these camps, their chances of reintegration into society are slim.

In parts of Nigeria, accusations of witchcraft have expanded to include children, often referred to as "child-witches." Evangelical preachers or self-proclaimed prophets who claim to detect witchcraft in children fuel this trend. These people inflict abuse, abandonment, and sometimes fatal exorcisms upon the accused children.

The witch-hunts in Africa again disproportionately target women, particularly older women and widows. This reflects the underlying gender dynamics that still pervade many African societies. These cultures often view women with limited social or economic power as easy scapegoats. Their victimization is often linked to the fear of independent women who do not conform to traditional roles. Jealousy or fear of women seen as a threat to the social order, especially those without male protectors, plays a role in their victimization.

Cultural and social norms that view women as inferior to men also explain the targeting of women in witch-hunts. In many African societies, cultural norms dictate women should be subservient to their husbands and male relatives. Society may view any deviation from these expectations as a threat to the social order. Society often views independent, educated, or economically powerful women with suspicion and may accuse them of witchcraft to control them. This cycle of violence and intimidation, stemming from such accusations, forces women to live in fear of persecution.

Traditional belief systems and modern religions play an overwhelmingly significant role in perpetuating witchcraft accusations. In many African societies, traditional belief systems coexist with modern religions, such as Christianity and Islam. Evangelical churches or charismatic leaders amplify fears of witchcraft by promoting the idea of spiritual warfare against witches and encouraging exorcisms or purges. These religious leaders may manipulate accusations to strengthen their own authority or attract followers by claiming to have the power to identify witches. Such accusations allow those in power to control others, portraying the accused as a danger to the village's spiritual health.

Local leaders or influential figures may also exploit witchcraft accusations to eliminate rivals or silence dissent. Accusing someone of being a witch can serve as a powerful tool for social or political control, especially in regions where belief in witchcraft remains widespread. Sometimes, local authorities or religious figures mobilize entire villages to attack individuals accused of witchcraft. This can lead to a situation condoning mob violence, the use of physical harm, or even death.

The lack of legal protections in many African countries allows mob violence against accused witches to go unpunished. Even in countries with laws against witchcraft accusations or witchhunts, enforcement is often inconsistent or ineffective because of deep-rooted cultural beliefs. This can create a culture of impunity, where individuals feel free to accuse and persecute others without fear of consequences. The result of this can be devastating, with many innocent people being accused and persecuted, and the social fabric of communities being torn apart.

Besides the lack of legal protections, the cultural and social norms that perpetuate witchcraft accusations also make it difficult to address the issue. Many people believe that witchcraft is a real and present danger to society. Witchcraft in African societies is not merely a relic of the past, but a living and growing phenomenon shaped by cultural, economic, and social forces. The fear of witchcraft continues to influence the dynamics of many communities, often with devastating consequences for the accused. While some government and non-government organizations have taken steps to combat witchcraft-related violence, the persistence of these practices highlights the need for deeper cultural understanding and systemic solutions. This is the only way to address the root causes of fear and suspicion. Understanding witchcraft in Africa requires recognizing its complexity is a blend of ancient traditions, modern challenges, and human struggles over power, resources, and identity.

South Asia

Modern witch-hunts remain a persistent issue in rural regions of South Asia, fueled by superstition, economic inequality, and social stratification. In these communities, deeply entrenched cultural beliefs about the supernatural make witchcraft accusations a powerful weapon. History shows that people often wield this weapon against society's most vulnerable members. Women, in particular, are subjected to these accusations, with widows, single women, and women from marginalized classes disproportionately targeted.

As we have repeatedly seen, these accusations frequently arise from disputes over scarce resources like land and water, as well as familial or community conflicts. In farming societies, land is a critical resource. Disputes over ownership or inheritance often result in accusations of witchcraft, particularly against women who stand in the way of a male relative's claim. Accusing a woman of being a witch provides a socially acceptable pretext to drive her out or even harm her to gain control of her property.

In parts of India, disputes related to dowry payments can also lead to witchcraft accusations. In-laws may label women whose families cannot fulfill dowry demands as witches, subjecting them to abuse or expulsion from the household.

Patriarchy, poverty, and superstition in rural South Asia explain these witch-hunts, which are not isolated incidents. Beyond the personal toll, they perpetuate cycles of marginalization and violence, reinforcing the precarious position of women in these communities.

Recognizing the severity of the issue, several Indian states have enacted laws aimed at curbing witch-hunts and protecting victims. One notable example is Jharkhand's *Prevention of Witch (Daain) Practices Act*, 2001. This law is a significant step towards addressing the problem of witch-hunts, as it criminalizes witchcraft accusations and related violence. The law imposes penalties for spreading superstitions or harming individuals under the guise of addressing witchcraft, which is a crucial measure in preventing further violence and intimidation.

Besides Jharkhand, other states, such as Bihar and Rajasthan, have also passed similar legislation to deter witch-hunts and provide justice for victims. These laws protect individuals from false accusations and related violence, and to promote a culture of tolerance and understanding. However, despite these efforts, enforcement of these laws remains inconsistent. Cultural beliefs that fuel witch-hunts often influence police and local authorities, who may therefore hesitate to intervene in cases of witchcraft accusations. This can be because of a variety of factors, including a lack of understanding of the laws and their implications, or a reluctance to challenge deeply ingrained cultural practices.

Still to this day, victims of witch-hunts often face significant barriers in seeking justice. Many of these individuals come from marginalized classes or tribal communities, who may lack access to legal resources or the confidence to seek justice. This may be because of a variety of factors, including a lack of education, poverty, or social isolation. As a result, victims may be reluctant to come forward and report cases of witchcraft accusations, which can perpetuate the cycle of violence and intimidation.

The challenges of enforcing these laws are further compounded by the complex cultural and social dynamics that underlie witch-hunts. In many Indian communities, witchcraft explains misfortune or illness, and accusations of witchcraft can justify violence and intimidation. Deeply ingrained cultural practices may make it difficult for authorities to intervene. The laws themselves may be inadequate or poorly enforced, which can perpetuate a culture of impunity and undermine efforts to address the problem of witch-hunts.

Despite these challenges, there are efforts underway to address witch-hunts in India. For example, some organizations are working to raise awareness about the laws and their implications, and to provide support and resources to victims of witch-hunts. There are efforts to promote cultural understanding and tolerance, and to challenge the deeply ingrained cultural practices that underlie witch-hunts.

While legal reforms are essential, social activism has played a crucial role in addressing the root causes of witch-hunts in South Asia. Non-governmental organizations (NGOs) and grassroots organizations are working tirelessly to combat the superstitions and social inequalities that enable these practices. By educating communities about the harms of witch-hunts and promoting scientific reasoning, activists aim to dispel myths about witchcraft and reduce fear-based accusations. NGOs provide legal help, shelter, and counseling for victims of witch-hunts, helping them rebuild their lives and reintegrate into society. Many of these organizations focus on empowering women through education, economic opportunities, and leadership training, addressing the gender inequality that underpins many witchcraft accusations.

Although modern witch-hunts are most commonly associated with regions like Africa and South Asia, they persist in other parts of the world as well. One such place is Papua New Guinea, where the belief in sorcery, "sanguma" is widespread and has led to horrific violence. In this country, accusations of sorcery are often used to explain misfortunes such as illness, death, or crop failure, and they frequently result in devastating consequences for the accused.

Victims of sorcery accusations in Papua New Guinea are again usually women, the elderly, or vulnerable individuals. Mobs, believing the accused, used supernatural powers to harm others, inflict brutal attacks, torture, and even murder them. Mobs often carry out these attacks in the name of community justice; however, in reality, they are vigilante violence fueled by fear, superstition, and a lack of understanding. The consequences of these attacks can be catastrophic, leaving families and communities shattered and traumatized.

The cultural context in which sorcery accusations occur in Papua New Guinea is complex and multifaceted. On the one hand, the belief in sorcery is deeply ingrained in the country's traditional culture, and it is often used to explain misfortunes and hardships. On the other hand, the modern challenges facing Papua New Guinea, such as urbanization and economic disparity, have intensified the problem of sorcery accusations. As communities under pressure turn to sorcery accusations to resolve conflicts or explaining misfortune, the risk of violence and intimidation increases.

In response to the problem of sorcery-related violence, the government of Papua New Guinea has taken steps to outlaw witchcraft-related violence. They have repealed laws that once recognized sorcery as a legal defense against another person.

However, enforcement remains weak, as local authorities often sympathize with the accusers or fear backlash from communities. This has bred a culture of impunity, where the perpetrators of violence rarely face consequences, and victims suffer silently.

Latin America

Witch-hunts in Latin America are less widespread or violent today compared to their historical peak in Europe or their modern manifestations in Africa, South Asia and Papua New Guinea. However, the belief in witchcraft and black magick remains deeply embedded in the cultural and spiritual fabric of the region. Particularly in rural areas and indigenous communities where fears surrounding supernatural powers continue to influence social interactions, sometimes leading to accusations and localized forms of persecution.

In many parts of Latin America, they view witchcraft, sorcery, and black magick as tangible forces that can influence health, relationships, and fortunes. Indigenous cosmologies and folk Catholicism often intertwine with these beliefs, framing witchcraft as both a source of healing and a cause of harm. While accusations of witchcraft today are less likely to result in physical violence than in other parts of the world, they can still have significant social consequences. Which includes items like ostracism, family rifts, and community-level disputes.

People in many Latin American communities, particularly in rural areas, believe that black magick involves rituals invoking malevolent spirits to harm others. Witches or sorcerers often receive the blame for misfortunes such as illness, financial losses, or failed harvests. Those accused of practicing black magick are often people perceived as outsiders, rivals, or individuals who challenge the community's norms. These accusations can be a means of reinforcing social solidarity by targeting individuals who deviate from accepted behaviors.

In countries like Mexico and Bolivia, where indigenous traditions and spiritual practices remain vibrant, witchcraft accusations continue to occur. In rural Mexican communities, the fear of "brujería" (witchcraft) persists, often intertwined with indigenous beliefs and folk Catholic practices. People believe witches, or "brujos/brujas," can cast curses, cause illnesses, or even control the weather.

Accusations may arise during conflicts within small communities, such as disputes over land, water, or personal relationships. While outright violence is rare, accused individuals may face social isolation, verbal harassment, or exclusion from any community rituals.

Oaxaca, in southern Mexico, and other similar regions have a rich tradition of spiritual healers or shamans. People often respect these practitioners but may also suspect them of using their knowledge for harmful purposes.

In Bolivia, people often intertwine accusations of witchcraft with the country's rich indigenous traditions, particularly those rooted in Andean cosmology. A profound respect for the spiritual realm and a recognition of the interconnectedness of all living beings characterizes this complex and multifaceted worldview. At the heart of this cosmology lies the concept of the "axis mundi," a sacred axis that connects the physical and spiritual worlds. Which is believed to be inhabited by a diverse array of supernatural beings, including witches, (brujos) and spiritual guides or shamans, (yatiris).

Many consider brujos powerful and feared figures who can wield both benevolent and malevolent forces. Some believe brujos can communicate with the spirits of the dead, diagnose and treat illnesses, and offer guidance and protection to those in need. However, people also fear them for their potential to cause harm and often accuse them of using their powers for malicious purposes. Yatiris earns reverence for their wisdom, spiritual insight, and ability to navigate the complex web of relationships between humans, animals, and the natural world.

In many Bolivian communities, people see practitioners embodying both qualities of brujos and yatiris, and they don't always clearly distinguish between them. This obscurity reflects the complex and nuanced nature of Andean spirituality, which recognizes the interconnectedness of all living beings. Providing potential for both good and evil to live within the same individual.

Despite the challenges posed by these accusations, many Bolivian communities continue to place a high value on traditional spiritual practices and the wisdom of their elders. Efforts to preserve and promote these traditions are underway, and there is a growing recognition of the importance of respecting and honoring the cultural heritage of Bolivia's indigenous peoples. Acknowledging and learning from the complex and multifaceted nature of Andean spirituality helps us understand how witchcraft accusations function as social control. It also shows us how traditional spiritual practices promote healing, justice, and reconciliation.

A key factor in the persistence of witchcraft beliefs in Latin America is the enduring role of indigenous spiritual practices. Many indigenous communities have their own forms of traditional healing, divination, and rituals, often led by their shamans, healers, or spiritual guides. These practitioners are intermediaries between the spiritual and physical worlds, capable of both curing illnesses and warding off malevolent forces.

People highly seek traditional healers known by various names depending on the region ("curanderos" in Mexico, "yatiris" in Bolivia, "payés" in Brazil), because of their ability to heal ailments and provide spiritual protection. However, their knowledge of rituals and herbs can also lead to suspicions that they might use their skills to harm others.

Many healers walk a fine line between being revered for their abilities and being feared for their potential misuse of spiritual power. Accusations of witchcraft sometimes target healers who fail to cure an ailment or are suspected of secretly aiding a rival or enemy. Witch-hunts, both historical and modern, reveal a universal human tendency to scapegoat individuals or groups during times of fear, uncertainty, or social upheaval. From the rural villages of Africa, South Asia, and the isolated communities of Papua New Guinea to the indigenous regions of Latin America, we can see how rooted they are in cultural beliefs. Believing this is where witchcraft and the supernatural intersect with issues such as poverty, gender inequality, resource disputes, and political instability.

While the specific forms and outcomes of witchcraft accusations vary widely across regions, the consequences are often devastating. Such as social out casting, physical violence, and the perpetuation of fear and superstition. Efforts to address these issues, such as legal reforms, grassroots activism, and education campaigns, have made progress in some areas. In other regions, significant challenges persist, especially where these beliefs are deeply ingrained in cultural and spiritual practices.

Today, modern technology and media have introduced additional dimensions to witch-hunts, enabling rumors to spread more rapidly and amplifying the reach and impact of accusations. This underscores the importance of tackling both the traditional and contemporary factors that fuel these harmful practices.

Ultimately, combating witch-hunts requires a multifaceted approach. One that combines legal protections, social support for victims, and cultural sensitivity with broader efforts to promote education, equity, and critical thinking. They must address the root causes of fear and superstition. While also addressing the socio-economic and political forces that sustain them, then societies can dismantle the structures that allow witch-hunts to persist. This global issue not only calls for local solutions but also serves as a reminder of the enduring power of belief and the human cost of marginalization and prejudice.

CHAPTER 15
STORIES OF INJUSTICE AND COURAGE

Throughout history, many individuals accused of witchcraft left behind interesting, often tragic stories. Their stories serve as a poignant reminder of the fear, superstition, and hysteria that characterized the witch trials. These cases not only highlight the deep-seated anxieties and misconceptions of their times, but also reflect the complex interplay of political, religious, and social pressures. After all, this is what eventually led to the downfall of the accused. In this chapter, we will examine four notable accused witches: Joan of Arc, Agnes Sampson, Ursula Kemp, and Katharina Kepler.

From the medieval streets of France to the rural villages of England, the lives of these four accused heretics and witches intersected with turbulent events of their respective eras. Eventually, authorities captured Joan of Arc, the young French heroine who led the charge against the English occupation and tried her for witchcraft and heresy. Her story shows the dangers of being a woman in a patriarchal society that blurred the lines between faith and madness.

King James VI of Scotland accused Agnes Sampson, a Scottish healer and midwife, of witchcraft. Her case highlights the tensions between traditional folk medicine and the emerging Protestantism of the time. Sampson's alleged use of magickal remedies and her connections to the Scottish nobility made her a target for persecution.

Ursula Kemp, an Englishwoman from the village of Manningtree, was one of the first women to be tried for witchcraft in the 16th century. Her story is a chilling example of how accusations of witchcraft could spread like wildfire through a community fueled by rumors, superstition, and personal vendettas.

Katharina Kepler was a resident of Leonberg, Württemberg Germany, and the mother of renowned astronomer Johannes Kepler. In 1615, authorities leveled accusations of witchcraft against Katharina Kepler, but her son defended her, resulting in her eventual release.

The stories of these four accused witches offer a nuanced and thought-provoking exploration of the complex social, cultural, and historical contexts that contributed to their tragic fates. By examining their cases, we gain a deeper understanding of how fear, superstition, and power can combine to destroy not only lives, but entire communities.

Joan of Arc

Joan of Arc, also known as the "Maid of Orléans," remains one of the most famous figures accused of heresy and witchcraft. Her story is a complex blend of faith, nationalism, and the intersecting forces of politics and religion during the violent period of the Hundred Years' War between England and France.

Now revered as a saint, her trial and execution in 1431 reflect how accusations of witchcraft were often a weapon to silence influential figures and discredit their causes.

She was a young peasant girl from Domrémy, France. She was born around 1412 in a small village nestled in the heart of the French countryside. Simplicity and hardship marked her early life, with no formal education to speak of. Yet, it was in this humble setting that Joan's extraordinary journey began.

At the tender age of thirteen, she claimed to have heard divine voices and experienced visions from Saint Michael, Saint Catherine, and Saint Margaret. She believed God's messages called her to help Charles VII, the disinherited French Dauphin, to win back his throne and free France.

The voices and visions that Joan received were a source of both comfort and confusion for her. On one hand, they provided her with a sense of purpose and direction, guiding her towards a path that would ultimately lead to greatness. On the other hand, they also made her a target of suspicion and ridicule among the townsfolk. Many saw her as a naïve and impressionable young girl, prone to flights of fancy and superstition. However, Joan remained resolute in her conviction, convinced that she was being called by a higher power to fulfill a sacred mission.

Initially, Joan sought an audience with Robert de Baudricourt, a local military commander who initially dismissed her. She persisted and eventually gained the support of two of Baudricourt's soldiers, Jean de Metz and Bertrand de Poulengy, who believed in her cause. Through these connections, Joan eventually secured an audience with Charles VII. Though reluctant at first, she convinced him of her divine mission and the importance of her role in reclaiming the French throne. Her persuasive arguments and unwavering conviction eventually won over the Dauphin, who saw her as a potential ally in his quest for power.

Historians claim she dressed in men's clothing for safety and to signify her role as a soldier, but the church did not agree. Joan led French troops to a series of astonishing victories, including the pivotal Battle of Orléans in 1429. Her success not only boosted French morale but also solidified Charles VII's position as the legitimate ruler.

The impact of Joan's victories was nothing short of remarkable. She became a national hero, celebrated by the French people for her bravery and determination. Her name was on everyone's lips, and her fame spread far and wide. However, her growing influence and the miraculous nature of her victories also aroused suspicion and resentment among both political and religious authorities.

To the English, Joan was a dangerous symbol of French resistance. They saw her as a threat to their own power and control over the region. To some within the French court, she was a potential threat to their own power and influence. A stark reminder that even the most unlikely of individuals could rise to greatness and challenge the status quo.

As Joan's star continued to shine, she found herself at the center of a maelstrom of intrigue and politics. Her enemies, both within and outside the French court, conspired against her, seeking to undermine her influence and discredit her claims of divine inspiration. A dramatic confrontation, leading ultimately to Joan's downfall and tragic fate, was about to begin. Despite the challenges and obstacles that lay ahead, Joan remained steadfast.

In 1430, the Burgundians, who were allies of the English, captured Joan during a mission to the besieged city of Compiègne. Her capture marked the start of her downfall. The Burgundians, who had long been at odds with the French, saw Joan as a valuable prize and a potential bargaining chip in their negotiations with the English. Instead of negotiating her release, Charles VII, the French king who had once hailed Joan as a hero, abandoned her, likely deeming her expendable since his coronation was secure. This betrayal was a crushing blow to Joan, who had risked everything to serve the French crown and had helped to secure its victory.

The Burgundians handed Joan over to the English, who sought to eliminate her as a political and, more importantly, a spiritual rallying point for the French. The English were determined to use her as a pawn in their game of politics, to discredit her and undermine the French resistance. Joan's downfall and tragic fate were set in motion by this impending dramatic and tragic confrontation.

The English held Joan's trial in Rouen, a city in northern France under their control. Pierre Cauchon, a pro-English bishop who presided over the trial proceedings, would ensure English interests were served. Cauchon was a ruthless and cunning man, who had no qualms about using underhanded tactics to achieve his goals. He was determined to secure a conviction against Joan, and he would do whatever it took to achieve that goal.

The charges against Joan were multifaceted, but they all revolved around accusations of heresy and witchcraft. The English and their allies claimed Joan was a heretic, a woman who had rejected the authority of the Church and was instead following her own path.

They accused her of claiming divine inspiration, of saying that she acted under the guidance of saints. The Church argued that these voices, which Joan believed were from God, could only come from Satan. They saw her as a woman possessed by the Devil, a woman who was under the control of evil forces.

The English also accused Joan of cross-dressing, of wearing male attire, which they saw as an abomination against God. They claimed this was a sign of her supposed pact with the Devil. A pact that had led her to reject the authority of the Church and to follow her own path. This charge was particularly egregious, as Joan had worn male attire for practical reasons, to protect herself from harm in military contexts. But the English were not interested in the truth; they were only interested in securing a conviction against her.

Joan's trial was a miscarriage of justice, designed to convict her from the outset. They denied her legal counsel, and they conducted the proceedings in Latin, a language she did not understand. Despite intense interrogation and threats of torture, Joan maintained her innocence, asserting that her visions were from God and that she acted in obedience to divine will.

The church tricked Joan into signing a confession in May 1431 by threatening to give her to the secular authorities for execution. However, she later recanted, reaffirming her faith in her visions. This act alone sealed her fate. The church handed Joan of Arc over to the secular authorities, and on May 30, 1431, they burned her at the stake in Rouen's marketplace. Witnesses reported that, as the flames consumed her, she called upon Jesus, and many in the crowd wept, viewing her as a martyr instead of a heretic.

Joan's story did not end with her tragic execution, it served as a catalyst for a profound shift in public sentiment. In the years that followed, the truth about her trial and conviction emerged. A growing number of people came to realize that she had been the victim of a grave injustice. By 1456, Pope Callixtus III, driven by a desire to rectify the wrongs of the past, ordered a retrial of Joan's case. This time, the court found her not guilty, declaring her trial a sham, a travesty of justice orchestrated by her enemies.

This reversal was not simply a matter of moral rectitude, but also a calculated move by Charles VII, the French king who had once hailed Joan as a hero. Now securely on the throne, he sought to erase the stain of heresy from his own legacy to distance himself from the controversy that had surrounded her. By declaring Joan innocent, Charles VII could whitewash his own role in her downfall and to present himself as a champion of justice and righteousness.

Centuries later, Joan's legacy continued to grow, and she became a powerful symbol of French nationalism and resilience. During the Napoleonic era, the French people hailed Joan as a heroine, a testament to their courage and determination in the face of adversity. And during both World Wars, the French people invoked her image as a reminder of their nation's rich history and its unwavering commitment to freedom and democracy.

Pope Benedict XV and the Catholic Church finally recognized Joan's unwavering faith and sacrifice in 1920 by canonizing her. This was a long-overdue recognition of her bravery and her devotion to her country, and it served as a testament to the enduring power of her legacy. Today, Joan of Arc remains one of the most revered figures in French history, a shining example of courage and conviction in the face of overwhelming odds.

Joan of Arc's story exemplifies how accusations of witchcraft and heresy could serve as a tool to suppress those who challenged the established power structures. While her visions and actions inspired awe among her followers, they were also deeply threatening to her enemies. Her trial highlights the dangerous intersection of 15th-century politics, religion, and gender, exposing how society labeled women who defied norms as both witches and heretics.

Agnes Sampson

Agnes Sampson's tragic story is a chilling example of the deadly consequences of Scotland's witch-hunting fervor during the late 16th century. Accusers charged Agnes, a respected healer and midwife, with witchcraft during the infamous North Berwick Witch Trials. These trials were a series of persecutions that reflected not only societal fears of witchcraft but also the personal paranoia of King James VI of Scotland.

Scotland, being deeply influenced by Calvinist Protestantism, viewed witchcraft as a direct threat to the moral and spiritual fabric of society. People thought witches used dark magick to cause misfortune, illness, and death.

The actions and beliefs of King James VI himself exacerbated this fear. James's deep fascination with and terror of witchcraft led him to view it as a real and present danger to his life and his kingdom. His fear intensified after his marriage to Anne of Denmark. In 1589, severe storms, which James interpreted as a witch-led conspiracy against him, disrupted Anne's voyage to Scotland. Upon investigating, he became convinced that witches in both Scotland and Denmark had plotted to kill them by summoning the storms.

It was in this climate of hysteria and royal obsession that the North Berwick Witch Trials began in 1590. The seaside town, where accused witches allegedly gathered, gave its name to these trials, marking it one of Scotland's first large-scale witch-hunts. Authorities accused dozens of people, mostly women, of participating in a demonic conspiracy against the king. Among them was a woman named Agnes Sampson.

Agnes Sampson was a midwife and healer from Haddington, East Lothian, a region nestled near the bustling city of Edinburgh. She lived a life that was both respected and precarious. As a woman with a deep understanding of herbal medicine and childbirth, she held a position of a great value in her community. However, this same knowledge and skill also made her a prime target for accusations of witchcraft. In the early modern society of Scotland, women like Agnes often walked a fine line between being valued for their expertise and being viewed with suspicion.

Their essential healing skills benefitted families and townsfolk, yet people blamed them for any unexplained misfortune like failed pregnancies, illnesses, or bad weather. Superstition and fear of the unknown ran deep during this period, blurring the lines between medicine and magick. Therefore, their knowledge of herbs and childbirth connected women like Agnes to the mysterious and unknown.

Agnes's reputation as a healer, combined with her status as an older, unmarried woman, made her a particularly vulnerable target for accusations of witchcraft. Agnes's independence and self-sufficiency stood out as unusual in a society defining women's roles by marital status. Her age also made her a suspect, as society often viewed older women with suspicion and believed them more likely to consort with the Devil. The fact she was unmarried and lived alone only added to the rumors and speculation that surrounded her.

Authorities in the North Berwick trials charged Agnes as a key conspirator in the alleged plot to kill King James VI. This was a period of great turmoil in Scotland, with the king's reign marked by power struggles, conflicts with England, and a deep-seated fear of witchcraft. Witchcraft preoccupied the king, and his court was rife with accusations and trials. Agnes, with her knowledge of herbs and her reputation as a healer, was an easy target for those seeking to gain favor with the King.

The charges against Agnes Sampson were sensational and deeply rooted in the prevailing fears of the time. Allegedly, Agnes used her magickal powers to summon storms that endangered King James VI and Queen Anne during their sea journeys.

Witnesses from the town claimed Agnes took part in a satanic ritual held in North Berwick. A sabbat of the sort, where witches reportedly pledged their loyalty to the Devil and plotted to harm the king. The charge against Agnes, like many accused witches, was causing illness and misfortune through curses and spells.

Confessions from other accused witches, many of whom named Agnes under torture, supposedly established her connection to the wider conspiracy. These confessions painted her as a leader within the alleged coven.

They arrested Agnes Sampson and brought her to the Holyrood Palace in Edinburgh, where her trial began. Her interrogation was brutal, marked by methods designed to extract confessions through both physical and psychological torture. Her interrogation included sleep deprivation, which was a common practice in Scottish witch trials. She was bound with a "witch's bridle," a device that clamped her mouth shut to prevent her from speaking. They also stripped and searched her for the "devil's mark," a physical sign (such as a mole or scar) that they believed was proof of a pact with the Devil. Interrogators would use any blemish on her body as evidence of her guilt.

Under this unbearable pressure and torture, Agnes confessed to the charges against her. She admitted to attending a witches' gathering at North Berwick, where witches supposedly danced, cast spells, and conducted unholy rituals. She also confessed to summoning storms to harm the king and his bride. Her confession, while clearly coerced, was used to validate the broader conspiracy theory embraced by King James VI and his advisors. Agnes's articulate and detailed accounts of witchcraft practices played into the fears of the time, further fueling the hysteria.

The court found Agnes Sampson guilty of witchcraft after her confession. The court sentenced her to death, like many accused witches. In early 1591, they hanged her and then burned her body at the stake. This method of execution was standard for Scottish witch trials, reflecting both the desire to punish witches and the belief that fire purified their souls.

Ursula Kemp

Ursula Kemp was a midwife and healer from the village of St. Osyth in Essex. She became one of the most infamous victims of England's witch trials in the late 16th century. Her story highlights the precarious position of women healers in a society that often viewed their knowledge of medicine and midwifery with suspicion. Accused of causing illness, death, and misfortune through witchcraft, Ursula's case shows how fear, personal vendettas, and cultural anxieties about gender and power could converge with devastating consequences.

As a single mother raising her illegitimate son, Thomas, she was already on the fringe of society at that time. Ursula relied on her skills as a healer to support her family. The community knew her well, and many townsfolk sought her help for ailments or childbirth complications.

However, her knowledge and independence made her a target of suspicion. They often viewed women like Ursula, who defied traditional gender roles and wielded knowledge of the body as dangerous or threatening. Accusations of witchcraft against healers often stemmed from interpersonal conflicts, professional rivalries, or failed expectations of care. In Ursula's case, a dispute with a former client, Grace Thurlow, who accused Ursula of using witchcraft to harm her and her family, was the basis of her charges.

The charges against Ursula Kemp began with a seemingly innocuous interpersonal grievance, but they quickly escalated into a full-blown witchcraft trial that would ultimately seal her fate. The catalyst for the accusations was Grace Thurlow, her neighbor who claimed that Ursula had caused the death of her infant child through sorcery. According to Thurlow, she had sought Ursula's help to cure the child of an illness, but when the child died, Thurlow alleged Ursula had cursed her family out of spite. This initial accusation was the spark that ignited a firestorm of accusations. It wasn't long before other townsfolk offered similar claims of Ursula's supposed magickal wrongdoing.

These accusations against Ursula were a tangled web of claims, each one more outlandish than the last. Villagers claimed she had bewitched their cows, causing them to fall ill and die. They accused her of using animal familiars, supernatural creatures believed to assist witches in their magickal practices, to cast spells and harm others. They described these familiars as a toad named "Pygine" and a cat named "Tyttey," Ursula's loyal companions in her supposed witchcraft. The villagers claimed these familiars were instrumental in Ursula's ability to cause harm, and that they were a key part of her magickal arsenal.

But the accusations against Ursula went beyond mere bewitchment and curses. Several townsfolk accused her of using spells and curses to inflict pain, lameness, and even death on those who crossed her. One of the most chilling aspects of Ursula's trial was her alleged admission that she could harm as well as heal. This dual role of both curing illnesses and supposedly causing them reflected the precarious position of healers in early modern England. Although people sought them for their skills, any perceived failure could result in deadly accusations. Those dissatisfied with Ursula's services, or who saw her as a threat to their own power, targeted her because of her reputation as a healer.

The accusations against Ursula were a classic example of the "witch-hunt" mentality that was prevalent in early modern England. Townsfolk were quick to blame her for any misfortune that befell them, and they would believe the most outlandish and fantastical claims about her supposed witchcraft. The trial that followed was a sham, with Ursula being subjected to intense pressure and coercion to confess to crimes that she may not have committed.

By the time of Kemp's trial in 1582, witchcraft accusations had become increasingly common in England. The 1563 Witchcraft Act, passed under Elizabeth I, criminalized witchcraft, making it punishable by death if harm occurred. This law reflected the growing concern about witches as agents of malice and disruption, both socially and spiritually.

The case against Ursula gained momentum when they brought her eight-year-old son, Thomas, forward as a witness. Under intense pressure and coercion, Thomas testified he had seen his mother speaking to her familiars and performing magickal acts. Accusers and juries in witch trials often accepted such testimony as firm evidence, even though it was unreliable and most likely fabricated. Using children as witnesses was a common tactic in these trials, believing they were less susceptible to suggestion and less likely to be influenced by external factors. Here, Thomas's testimony was a crucial piece of evidence that helped to build the case against his own mother.

As the trial against Ursula continued, her accusers subjected her to one of the most infamous methods of determining guilt, the "swimming test." If the individual floated, it was a proof of guilt, believing that holy water rejected witches. If they sank, they were innocent but could still drown. This method was a clear example of the superstition and ignorance that characterized the witch trials of the time. Thinking water could somehow reveal a person's guilt or innocence was a product of medieval folklore, and it was a testament to the desperation and fear that drove the witch-hunters.

Ursula reportedly floated during this ordeal, sealing her fate in the eyes of her accusers. Her floating convinced her accusers of her guilt, justifying her conviction. The "swimming test" was a cruel and inhumane practice that was often used to extract confessions from accused witches. By placing them in water, the authorities hoped to break their spirits and extract a confession, even if it was false. In Ursula's case, the "swimming test" was a turning point in the trial, and it helped to seal her fate.

Following her "failed" "swimming test" and the confessions extracted from others under duress, they convicted Ursula of witchcraft. Her trial implicated several other women in St. Osyth, leading to a cascade of accusations and executions. The witch-hunt that followed was a tragic example of how fear, superstition, and misinformation can lead to devastating consequences.

In rural communities like St. Osyth, witchcraft often attributed to many unexplained misfortunes such as the death of livestock, failed harvests, or sudden illnesses. Religious changes following the English Reformation, which had heightened anxieties about the Devil's influence in daily life, amplified this fear. Protestant Church leaders stressed the idea of witches' alliance with Satan, thus further stigmatizing those suspected of magick or supernatural abilities.

Midwives and healers, like Ursula, occupied a particularly vulnerable position in this climate. Although they provided essential services, their work often involved life-and-death situations, such as childbirth or illness, with uncertain outcomes. When tragedies occurred, these women could easily become scapegoats for a community's grief or anger.

Katharina Kepler

In the early 17th century, Katharina Kepler found herself at the center of a witch trial in the small German town of Ellwangen. She was the mother of renowned astronomer Johannes Kepler.

Initially, she had been a vocal opponent of witchcraft accusations in her community, speaking out against the hysteria and fear that gripped the village. However, her defiance and outspoken nature ultimately made her a target, and she soon found herself accused of the very crimes she had once so strongly condemned.

In 1615, a series of events unfolded that would ultimately lead to the downfall of Katharina, a woman whose life was about to take a drastic turn. A former friend, consumed by chronic pain and desperation, made the unfounded accusation that Katharina, a known herbalist, had caused their suffering through magickal drinks. This baseless claim sparked a chain reaction, as neighbors and townsfolk offered their own tales of dark magick, spells, and poisoning. Thick with suspicion and fear in the air, Katharina's reputation was about to irreparably harmed.

As the accusations mounted, Katharina's life became increasingly isolated. The once-peaceful community was now gripped by hysteria, with many believing that Katharina was a malevolent force to be reckoned with. The local authorities, fueled by the fervor of the crowd, took notice of the situation, and Katharina's fate was all but sealed. They arrested her on August 7, 1620, throwing into a dark, damp cell, awaiting trial for the heinous crime of witchcraft. The road ahead would be long and treacherous, and Katharina's future hung precariously in the balance.

The accusations against Katharina continued to mount. Her son Johannes Kepler, a renowned astronomer and mathematician, found himself at a crossroads. With his scientific career in full swing, Kepler had been making groundbreaking discoveries in the field of astronomy, but he knew he couldn't ignore the plight of his mother. He put his work on hold, dedicating himself to gathering evidence and building a case to clear her name. Kepler's defense was a testament to his unwavering dedication to his mother and his unshakeable commitment to pursuing the truth.

With a keen mind and a sharp intellect, Kepler set out to interview the witnesses, gather testimony, and present a spirited defense of his mother's innocence. He pored over the evidence, searching for any inconsistencies or flaws in the prosecution's case. As he delved deeper into the matter, Kepler became increasingly convinced that his mother was the victim of a malicious conspiracy, rather than a genuine witch. With his reputation as a scientist and a scholar, Kepler was well-equipped to challenge the superstitions and misconceptions that had led to his mother's arrest.

In 1621, Kepler's tireless efforts finally succeeded, and the court acquitted Katharina. Her trial was a rare instance of a son defending his mother against accusations of witchcraft. Johannes Kepler's actions served as a powerful testament to the importance of standing up for what is right, even in the face of overwhelming opposition. Through his bravery and determination, Kepler had saved his mother from a fate worse than death and had also helped to shed light on the darker aspects of human nature.

CHAPTER 16
URBAN GRANDIER AND THE URSULINE NUNS

The 17th century in Europe was a time of profound religious fervor, political intrigue, and social turbulence. France, in particular, was navigating the complexities of the Counter-Reformation, where the Catholic Church sought to reaffirm its authority in the face of Protestantism. It was also a period rife with superstition, fear of witchcraft, and a belief in demonic possession. All of which were deeply embedded in the collective consciousness of society. Against this backdrop, one of the most infamous cases of alleged possession and witchcraft unfolded in the small French town of Loudun. This was the case of Urbain Grandier and the possession of the Ursuline nuns, a story that remains one of the most controversial and debated episodes in European history.

At the heart of the affair was Urbain Grandier, a Catholic priest of remarkable charisma, intelligence, ambition, and good looks. Grandier, however, was also a divisive figure, known for his defiance of authority, his rumored moral indiscretions, and his political and personal rivalries. He became the focal point of accusations of witchcraft when a group of Ursuline nuns in

Loudun claimed to be possessed by demons and named him as their tormentor.

His case is a fascinating example of how the Catholic Church and the French monarchy joined forces to eliminate perceived threats to their power. Grandier's alleged demonic possession and his connections to the local nobility made him a convenient scapegoat for the troubles plaguing the town.

The possession of the Ursuline nuns and the trial of Urbain Grandier were more than an isolated event. It was emblematic of the broader cultural, religious, and political dynamics of the 17th century. The interplay of power, fear, and superstition in this affair sheds light on the mechanisms of control exercised by both religious and secular authorities. The case raises timeless questions about mass hysteria, the role of personal and political vendettas, and the human tendency to scapegoat in times of uncertainty.

As we unravel this tale, we see that the story of Urbain Grandier and the Ursuline possessions is not merely one of alleged witchcraft and exorcism. It is a lens through which we can better understand the intersection of faith, power, and human psychology during a pivotal era in European history.

17th century France was an era marked by religious, political, and social upheaval. The Catholic Church, having lost ground to the Protestant Reformation, launched the Counter-Reformation. This was a sweeping campaign by the Catholic Church to reassert its dominance in Europe. The French monarchy, which sought to use Catholicism as a unifying force to merge its power, supported this religious revival. Against this backdrop, the line between spiritual and political authority blurred, with accusations of witchcraft and demonic possession often serving as tools for social and political control.

The Catholic Church's Counter-Reformation efforts intensified in France following the Edict of Nantes in 1598, which granted religious tolerance to Protestants (Huguenots). While the edict aimed to reduce sectarian conflict, it created lingering tensions between Catholics and Protestants. By the early 1600s, the monarchy, under King Louis XIII and guided by his powerful chief minister Cardinal Richelieu, prioritized reinforcing Catholic unity to strengthen the state. Promoting religious orthodoxy was not just as a matter of faith but a cornerstone of political stability.

This period also saw a renewed emphasis on combating heresy and purging perceived threats to the Church. Institutions like the Inquisition were active in rooting out deviance, including witchcraft and demonic possession, which were viewed as manifestations of heretical or satanic forces. The Church's focus on maintaining ideological purity created an environment in which accusations of witchcraft and possession flourished. This provided a means of targeting individuals or groups deemed troublesome.

Demonic possession usually involved accusations of sexual impropriety and pacts with the Devil, reflecting broader anxieties about morality and social order. Women, particularly those in positions of vulnerability or authority, were frequent targets of such accusations. Convents, as enclosed religious spaces, became fertile ground for rumors of possession, especially when coupled with political or personal disputes.

The Loudun affair unfolded during the tenure of Cardinal Richelieu, one of the most influential figures in French history. As Louis XIII's chief minister, Richelieu wielded immense power, shaping both French domestic and foreign policy. He was determined to centralize authority and suppress any challenges to the monarchy, whether they came from rebellious nobles, Protestant enclaves, or independent-minded clergy like Urbain Grandier.

Accusations of possession allowed Church authorities to assert their control over convents and their inhabitants. Possession narratives often involved themes of sexual temptation and moral corruption, reflecting broader fears about women's sexuality and its potential to disrupt societal order. In Loudun, these anxieties steeped the accusations against Urbain Grandier and the nuns. With the alleged possession serving as both a metaphor for and a literalization of perceived moral and spiritual disorder.

Urbain Grandier was born in 1590 in the French town of Bouère to a relatively modest but respectable family. His intelligence and charisma set him apart at an early age, allowing him to pursue higher education at the University of Poitiers. There, he studied theology, receiving the training necessary to enter the priesthood. Grandier's eloquence, charm, and striking appearance made him a natural orator and a prominent figure in clerical circles. However, it was these same qualities that would later contribute to his downfall, as they earned him powerful enemies and a reputation for arrogance and immorality.

In 1617, the Jesuits granted Grandier two lucrative benefices. Upon his arrival in Loudun, he became the parish priest of Saint-Pierre-du-Marché and appointed as canon at the Church of Sainte-Croix. Almost immediately, his tenure in Loudun became controversial. Known for his eloquent sermons and his ability to attract large congregations, Grandier quickly gained a reputation as a compelling preacher. Many admired him for his intellect and charisma, but others viewed him as too prideful and ambitious.

At the young age of twenty-seven, the elegant Grandier was handsome and notably eloquent, with a calm manner, sharp wit, and glamour to spare. Although he had made enemies, he also had earned the support of many influential men early in his career.

Grandier was not a man who shied away from confrontation. He openly criticized the practices of his fellow clergy, often accusing them of corruption and hypocrisy. This antagonized many of his peers, who resented his self-perceived moral superiority. Furthermore, his refusal to conform to ecclesiastical norms and his defiance of Church hierarchy alienated him from influential figures within the diocese.

While Grandier's intellectual brilliance and rhetorical skills earned him admirers, his personal life became the subject of scandalous rumors. Despite his vow of celibacy, the townsfolk accused him of having sexual relationships with multiple women in Loudun, including laywomen and nuns. These allegations, whether true or exaggerated, contributed significantly to his reputation as a corrupt and immoral priest.

One of the most notorious accusations involved his relationship with Philippe Trincant, the daughter of the local prosecutor, Jean Trincant. Grandier reportedly seduced Philippe, and their affair became a source of public outrage. After Philippe became pregnant, the scandal humiliated Jean Trincant. This is when he became one of Grandier's most vocal enemies, joining a growing faction of individuals eager to see the priest discredited and punished.

Another prominent affair attributed to Grandier involved Madeleine de Brou, a wealthy and influential widow. Although Madeleine initially sought spiritual guidance from Grandier, their relationship allegedly deepened into a romantic and sexual liaison. This further scandalized the community and provided additional ammunition for his accusers, who portrayed him as a libertine unworthy of his clerical position.

Grandier's relationships with women extended beyond personal affairs to professional conflicts, particularly with the Ursuline nuns of Loudun. A relatively new religious order, the Ursuline Sisters, had opened its first convent in Loudun in 1626. In 1632, the young Jeanne des Anges became prioress, leading a convent of seventeen similarly youthful nuns averaging twenty-five years old. Mother Jeanne des Anges later became the central figure in the possession narrative.

Urban Grandier's troubles extended beyond personal scandals. He was also involved in a complex network of political and ecclesiastical rivalries. One of his most significant adversaries was Cardinal Richelieu, the powerful chief minister of France. While Richelieu did not initially target Grandier, their paths crossed because of Grandier's opposition to the crown's plans to demolish Loudun's fortifications. Richelieu, seeking to centralize power and suppress potential rebellions, viewed the fortifications as a threat to royal authority, while Grandier and others in Loudun argued for their preservation.

Grandier's opposition to Richelieu's policies, coupled with his reputation as a troublemaker, made him a convenient target for suppression. Richelieu's influence caused those accusing Grandier to be taken seriously by the church, regardless of the validity of the accusations.

Grandier had even alienated local clergy and church authorities with his criticism and nonconformity. These rivalries ensured that when accusations of witchcraft emerged, there would be no shortage of individuals willing to testify against him or support his prosecution.

By the late 1620s, Grandier's enemies had conspired against him more openly. In 1629, accusations of immorality and defamation resulted in his first trial, where the court found him guilty. In the wake of this devastating decision, Grandier and his allies worked diligently to restore his livelihood and reputation. Later, Grandier and his allies presented his case to the Parlement of Paris, which then referred it to the court at Poitiers. Many of the witnesses against Grandier retracted their statements, perhaps because they felt uncomfortable about lying before a royal court. The court set aside the case against Grandier, leaving it open. This initial trial, however, planted the seeds for the later, more serious accusations of witchcraft.

This all changed just after the plague began in 1632, when the Ursuline nuns of Loudun began exhibiting symptoms of demonic possession. The nuns, led by Mother Jeanne des Anges, claimed to be tormented by spirits who accused Urbain Grandier of being the source of their affliction. According to their testimonies, Grandier had entered into a pact with the Devil and used sorcery to send demons to possess the nuns. Dramatic displays of possession, including fits, contortions, and speaking in tongues, which were all interpreted as evidence of a supernatural influence, bolstered these accusations.

The possessions started with a junior nun, Sister Marthe. Who claimed she had a vision of Father Moussaut, the nun's recently deceased confessor. The visions of Father Moussaut soon transformed into erotic visions of Urbain Grandier, whom the nuns themselves had never met. Lustful dreams of Grandier spread among the nuns, including Mother Jeanne des Anges.

Mother des Anges claimed she was being tormented by a demon named Asmodeus, known in Christian demonology as the demon of lust. She alleged Asmodeus had entered her body and was attempting to corrupt her soul. Other nuns reported similar experiences, with several claiming shadowy figures had attacked them or that they saw them moving about.

Initially, the events remained within the convent walls. However, as the number of afflicted nuns grew, word of the possessions spread throughout Loudun. The spectacle drew the attention of local clergy and townsfolk alike, many of whom came to witness the strange occurrences for themselves. This marked the beginning of what would become a public sensation.

The turning point in the possession narrative came when the nuns identified Urbain Grandier as the cause of their torment. Mother des Anges claimed that Grandier had used sorcery to send demons to possess her and the other nuns. She cited his supposed ability to wield supernatural powers as evidence of his guilt. According to the nuns, Grandier had made a pact with the Devil, granting him dark and malevolent powers in exchange for his very soul. They said Grandier sealed this alleged pact with a series of sinister rituals, performed in secret.

The nuns' dramatic behavior, including their reported trances during exorcisms and frenzied cries of Grandier's name, supported the accusations against him. The nuns claimed Grandier had summoned the demons inhabiting their bodies and used magickal objects to enchant them. These objects rendered them helpless against the forces of darkness. Authorities believed the nuns' behavior manifested the demons' presence, their bodies contorting unnaturally and their voices taking on a menacing, otherworldly tone.

This attracted the attention of exorcists from across the region. Among the most prominent was Father Jean-Joseph Surin, a Jesuit priest renowned for his work in combating possession.

Surin and other exorcists conducted public exorcism rituals within the convent, during which time the nuns exhibited their dramatic behavior. The lewd and bizarre behavior of the young nuns during the exorcisms attracted an ever-increasing audience. The nuns shouted expletives, barked, exposed themselves, spoke a garbled form of Latin, and contorted their bodies into obscene positions.

The exorcisms became public spectacles, drawing enormous crowds eager to witness the struggle between good and evil. The nuns' behavior, combined with the authority of the exorcists, convinced many that the possessions were genuine. Skeptics, however, noted that the symptoms exhibited by the nuns often mirrored the descriptions found in popular demonological texts of the time. This might suggest someone may have fabricated or manipulated the possessions.

Eventually, this became such a spectacle, the Crown and Cardinal Richelieu intervened. A desire to maintain stable relations between the Huguenots and the Catholics in Loudun may have sparked their decision to bring the royal presence to bear. The exorcisms did not seem to work, and it's probable they concluded that a priest's seduction of a parishioner was conduct too inappropriate to ignore. On a personal level, Richelieu had suffered a humiliating public slight by Grandier some years before his ascent to power as the King's first minister. Whatever the reasons for taking an interest in the affair, the Crown's intervention sealed Grandier's fate.

Following the accusations from the Ursuline nuns, authorities arrested and imprisoned Urbain Grandier. The authorities leveled severe charges against him. They accused him of sorcery, a pact with the Devil, and using demonic forces to possess the nuns. These allegations, while dramatic, were not without precedent. Throughout Europe, witchcraft trials often involved claims of diabolical pacts and supernatural influence.

His many enemies orchestrated Grandier's arrest, including Cardinal Richelieu, who saw the trial as an opportunity to eliminate a political adversary. Jean Trincant, the local prosecutor and one of Grandier's most vocal detractors, also played a key role in pushing the case forward. The personal and political vendettas intertwined deeply with the charges, which, on the surface, stemmed from religious concerns.

The investigation into Grandier's alleged crimes began with a series of intense interrogations of the nuns and exorcists involved in the case. The nuns, led by the enigmatic and fervent Mother Jeanne des Anges, repeated their claims that Grandier had bewitched them, sending demons to torment them with unrelenting ferocity. They described him as a sorcerer who had made a pact with the Devil to gain power and influence. They claimed he had used his supposed magickal abilities to manipulate and control them.

As the investigation continued, investigators also turned their attention to searching for physical evidence of witchcraft. According to the prevailing superstitions of the time, witchhunters believed that witches often bore "devil's-marks" on their bodies where demons had touched or marked them. These marks served as evidence of the witch's guilt and were believed to be proof of a pact with the Devil.

They subjected Grandier to a humiliating physical examination, during which they searched his body for such marks. The examination was a degrading and dehumanizing experience, with Grandier being forced to submit to a series of invasive and uncomfortable procedures. They probed and searched his body, examining his skin for any sign of the devil's touch. Although they found no conclusive devil's-marks, the examination further convinced the public of Grandier's guilt. The image of the accused sorcerer, stripped bare and subjected to the indignities of a physical examination, was a powerful one. One that helped to solidify the public's perception of Grandier as a servant of the Devil.

One of the most infamous pieces of "evidence" presented against Grandier was a supposed demonic pact written in Latin and signed by Grandier and several demons. Prosecutors widely publicized this document, which appeared later during Grandier's trial, as a proof of his guilt, although its authenticity was highly questionable. The pact purportedly detailed Grandier's agreement to serve the Devil and his minions. The pact detailed a series of dark and twisted rituals that Grandier allegedly performed to seal his pact. Despite the lack of concrete evidence, the pact was a damning indictment of Grandier's character and used by his accusers to paint him as a servant of the Devil.

They conducted Grandier's trial before a specially appointed tribunal rather than a standard court. This tribunal, heavily influenced by Richelieu and local authorities, was far from impartial. Many members had ties to Grandier's enemies, thus biasing the proceedings from the start.

The trial was rife with irregularities. Witnesses against Grandier included not only the nuns but also local townsfolk who claimed to have seen him engaging in suspicious activities. However, much of the testimony was contradictory or based on hearsay. Grandier was also denied the right to cross-examine witnesses, severely limiting his ability to mount any defense.

Despite the lack of concrete evidence, the tribunal was determined to convict Grandier. His eloquence and intelligence, which had often served him well in the past, were now used against him. With prosecutors portraying him as a cunning manipulator capable of deceiving even the most devout.

Urbain Grandier maintained his innocence throughout the trial. He vehemently denied the accusations of witchcraft and sorcery. Arguing he was the victim of a conspiracy orchestrated by his political and religious rivals. He pointed out the inconsistencies in the testimony against him and highlighted the absurdity of the claims, such as the alleged demonic pact.

Grandier's defense, however, fell on deaf ears. The tribunal was not interested in uncovering the truth, but in securing a conviction. His refusal to confess only hardened the resolve of his accusers, who viewed his denials as further evidence of his guilt.

After months of proceedings, the tribunal found Urbain Grandier guilty of witchcraft and heresy. The court sentenced him to be burned alive, a punishment reserved for the most severe cases of heresy and sorcery. They announced the verdict with great fanfare, and preparations for the execution began immediately.

The Church intended such a sentence not only as punishment for Grandier but also as a public demonstration of its power and commitment to combating evil. The execution was staged as a spectacle, designed to reinforce the authority of religious and secular leaders.

On August 18, 1634, they led Urbain Grandier to the stake in Loudun's town square to burn him alive. Authorities attempted to extract a confession by torturing him before his execution, but he steadfastly maintained his innocence. Eyewitnesses reported Grandier prayed fervently and faced his death with dignity, further fueling the belief among some that he was a martyr rather than a sorcerer.

As the flames consumed him, the crowd watched in horror and fascination. For his supporters, his death was a miscarriage of justice. For his accusers, it was a necessary act to purge Loudun of evil.

However, the possessions did not end with Grandier's gruesome death. The last exorcism took place in 1638, following the continuation of the events with the nuns. At the trial, both church and state declared the nuns possessed. Only later did people believe the church may have selected the nuns to endure the possessions for its glory.

In the years following Grandier's death, doubts about the trial and its legitimacy grew. Mother Jeanne des Anges, the chief accuser, later claimed to have experienced a miraculous healing and declared that Grandier had forgiven her from beyond the grave. Her claims added another layer of mystery to the case, raising questions about her motivations and the authenticity of the possessions.

Mother Jeanne des Anges later admitted to harboring a personal grudge against Grandier, possibly because of an earlier rejection of the convent. Whether or not this grudge was the true origin of the possession narrative, Grandier's enemies seized it as an opportunity to destroy him.

The case of Urbain Grandier and the possession of the Ursuline nuns of Loudun is a tragic and complex episode that reflects the turbulent dynamics of 17th-century France. At its heart, it is a story of intersecting forces: religion, politics, personal vendettas, and mass hysteria. These forces combined to create a spectacle that led to the persecution and eventual execution of an intelligent but polarizing figure, whose guilt or innocence remains debated to this day.

Grandier's charisma and defiance made him a target in a society where conformity to religious and political authority was paramount. The accusations of witchcraft against him were emblematic of an era in which fear of the supernatural and the Devil was pervasive. Authorities interpreted the Ursuline nuns' alleged possessions, marked by dramatic displays of hysteria and claims of demonic influence, not only a moral crisis. In it, they found an opportunity to reassert control over an increasingly troublesome society.

The trial and execution of Urban Grandier reveal the extent to which personal rivalries and political ambitions could subvert justice. The involvement of powerful figures like Cardinal Richelieu underscores how intertwined religious institutions were with the state's power. For Richelieu, the destruction of Grandier was a means of consolidating authority, silencing dissent, and reinforcing Catholic orthodoxy. For the local clergy and townsfolk, it was an opportunity to eliminate a controversial figure who had long divided the community.

Modern interpretations of the Loudun affair suggest the possessions were likely a product of psychological and social factors rather than supernatural forces. The restrictive environment of the Ursuline convent, combined with the personal struggles of Mother Jeanne des Anges and the pressures of the time, created conditions ripe for collective hysteria. Grandier, with his reputation for defiance and scandal, became an ideal scapegoat.

CHAPTER 17
LEGACIES OF THE PERSECUTED

In the shadowy annals of human history, there are few chapters as chilling as those chronicling the witch-hunts. From the windswept plains of medieval Europe to the growing colonies of America, waves of paranoia swept through communities, leaving devastation in their wake. The accused were more often than not just ordinary individuals. Baseless claims of consorting with the Devil uprooted mothers, daughters, neighbors, and even respected members of society. Superstition and fear of the unknown fueled these accusations, and societal norms of the time perpetuated them. Though centuries have passed, the echoes of their suffering remain vivid, serving as haunting reminders of the destructive power of fear and ignorance.

The witch trials occurred across various times and places. They were a phenomenon born from deeply ingrained social anxieties. At their core, they reflected a dangerous combination of religious fervor, misogyny, and social strife. The witch-hunts were often a manifestation of the societal tensions of the time, with women being disproportionately targeted because of their perceived vulnerability to demonic influence. The trials were often a tool for the powerful to assert their dominance over the weak, with the accused being subjected to cruel and inhumane treatment. For those ensnared in this frenzy, there was little hope of escape. Accusations that were often absurd tore apart their lives, and trials that were little more than a facade of justice decided their fates.

Their lack of due process and the use of dubious evidence, such as "spectral evidence" and "swim tests", characterized the witch trials. They often subjected the accused to physical torture, including being burned at the stake, hanged, or broken on the wheel. The trials were often a spectacle, with the accused being paraded through the streets, and the townsfolk being encouraged to take part in the "justice" being meted out.

The witch-hunts that gripped Europe, North America, and other parts of the world did not discriminate along the lines of personality, profession, or morality. While the accusations often targeted specific demographics like women, the elderly, and the marginalized, the victims were, in reality, as diverse as the societies they lived in. Each accusation, trial, and execution involved a complex interplay of personal, social, and political factors.

Women were overwhelmingly the primary targets of the witch-hunters, reflecting the deeply ingrained misogyny of the societies where witch-hunts thrived. Yes, they accused men too, particularly in Finland, but at the heart of these accusations lay a fear of female autonomy. Especially for women who dared to live outside societal norms. Older widows, single mothers, childless women, or those who defied expectations by engaging in professions such as healing or midwifery were vulnerable.

Authorities often saw these women as a threat to the patriarchal order, suspecting their independence and self-sufficiency. The fact many of these women were also skilled in traditional healing practices, which were often passed down through generations of women, only added to their perceived threat.

A deep-seated fear of female power and a desire to control women's bodies and lives often fueled the accusations against women. Women accused of witchcraft were often those who had lived outside the boundaries of traditional feminine roles, such as being educated, independent, or having a strong sense of self. The witch-hunts were a tool for the patriarchal societies to assert their dominance over women and to suppress any form of female autonomy. The consequences of these accusations were devastating, with many women being tortured, imprisoned, or executed for crimes they did not commit.

Besides women, witch-hunters also targeted other marginalized groups, such as the elderly, the poor, and people with disabilities. Seeing these individuals as outsiders, their perceived vulnerability, made them easy targets for accusations.

In Germany, the Würzburg Witch Trials of the early 17th century saw a shocking number of children accused and executed. Executioners burned over 40 children at the stake, often accusing them of participating in witch sabbats or practicing sorcery. These trials were driven by a combination of religious fanaticism and local politics, with children's confessions extracted under extreme torture. Their deaths remain one of the most horrifying aspects of the European witch-hunts.

Dorothy Good, a four-year-old girl, was the youngest person accused during the Salem Witch Trials. Authorities arrested her and her mother, Sarah Good, and they spent months in jail under appalling conditions. Her innocence and age did not shield her from the hysteria; witch-hunters coerced her into confessing that her mother bewitched her. Although Dorothy's release eventually came, her imprisonment left lasting scars. Her story illustrates the indiscriminate nature of the trials and the vulnerability of children in the face of societal madness.

Bridget Bishop was the first person executed during the Salem Witch Trials of 1692. She became a symbol of how societal biases could seal the fate of an outspoken individual. Bridget was a middle-aged woman known for her vibrant personality, colorful clothing, and tendency to challenge societal norms. She owned a tavern and was independent, a rarity in Puritan New England. Her independent streak, combined with her reputation for marital strife and prior accusations of witchcraft, made her an easy scapegoat. At her trial, spectral evidence was used to convict her. Bridget's story underscores the precariousness of being a woman who stood out in a society obsessed with conformity and piety.

In England, Agnes Waterhouse was among the first women executed for witchcraft. In 1566, they accused her of casting spells to kill livestock and people. Her admission to owning a familiar spirit, a demonic cat named "Sathan," further incriminated her. Her eventual execution was not just the result of superstition but a reflection of the fears surrounding the community. A Fear of women who had access to practical knowledge, such as herbal remedies or animal husbandry.

Katharina Henot of Cologne is one of the most notable victims of the witch trials in 17th-century Germany. She was a successful postmaster, which was an uncommon position for a woman in those times. Henot had carved out a place for herself in a male-dominated profession. Her leadership and independence, however, made her a target in a society deeply uneasy with women wielding power. Accused of using witchcraft to sabotage competitors and spread illness, Henot maintained her innocence even under torture. In 1627, authorities executed her, making her death a symbol of how professional jealousy and societal biases can destroy lives.

Maria Holl's story is a remarkable one of defiance and resilience. Accused of witchcraft in 1593 in the town of Nördlingen, Germany, Maria endured repeated bouts of torture designed to force a confession. Unlike many others, Maria refused to confess to crimes she had not committed, even under immense physical and psychological pressure. Her steadfastness eventually saved her life. Because they could produce no evidence beyond accusations, and they released her. Maria's story is exceptional since most victims either confessed under duress or perished. She stands as a powerful testament to the courage of those who resisted the machinery of persecution.

Merga Bien was a German woman living in Bamberg during the infamous witch trials of the 1620s and was another tragic casualty of this era. Unlike many victims, Merga was neither impoverished nor marginalized. She was married to a wealthy merchant and lived a comfortable life. However, her inability to conform to societal expectations made her a target. They accused her of murdering her first two husbands and of using sorcery to harm others. Merga's greatest "crime" was her assertiveness and outspokenness. Even her pregnancy, which was a status that should have spared her execution under Church law, did not save her. In 1627, executioners burned Merga alive, leaving behind a legacy of how society criminalized social nonconformity under the guise of witchcraft.

Baseless and varied accusations fueled the Salem witch trials. Young girls claimed to be afflicted by "witches," pointing fingers at neighbors with little more than their own hysterical testimony. A mix of superstition, fear, and personal vendettas often fueled the accusations. Elsewhere, people often rooted accusations in convenience, using the witch-hunts to settle scores or eliminate rivals. A crop failure, a stillbirth, or an unexplained illness could all serve as catalysts for claims of witchcraft, with the accused being blamed for the misfortune.

We previously discussed Agnes Sampson, the midwife, accused of causing a storm that endangered King James VI's voyage. The accusation was a classic example of the absurdity of the charges and the lengths to which authorities would go to extract confessions. They forced Sampson, under torture, to confess to summoning the tempest with "witchcraft". Her story, like so many others, illustrates the desperation and fear that drove people to make such outlandish accusations. The fact Sampson was a respected member of her community, a skilled midwife who had helped countless women bring new life into the world, made her accusation even more shocking.

Iceland's short-lived witchcraft panic went against the grain of the time as they disproportionately accused men. Against this backdrop, Thorgeir Gudmundsson's story stands out. Based on vague testimonies of him harming a neighbor's livestock with magick, they convicted Thorgeir of sorcery. Iceland's witch trials, unlike those in other parts of Europe, focused heavily on accusations against men. This anomaly stemmed from the country's folklore, which associated magick with learned practices passed down through generations, often among male practitioners known as "wise men."

We cannot overstate the psychological impact on the accused. Authorities subjected many to brutal interrogations, stripping them of their dignity and forcing them to endure public shaming. The situation often pulled families into the conflict, damaging their reputations through association. The accused often endured physical and emotional torture at the hands of their captors. This included being subjected to things like "witch-pricking" to determine if a person had any physical marks that were believed to be signs of a pact with the Devil. Coercion and intimidation often extracted confessions from the accused, who were forced to confess to crimes they did not commit.

For those who survived the trials, life would never be the same. The trials left many with both physical and emotional scars while ruining their reputations. Their communities often shunned them, forcing them to live on the fringes of society. The trauma of the trials could last a lifetime, with many survivors struggling to rebuild their lives and restore their dignity.

The trials themselves were grim spectacles, more akin to sideshow performances than genuine attempts at justice. The trials often lacked evidence or had deeply flawed evidence, and the kangaroo court system subjected the accused to predetermined outcomes. Prosecutors cited moles or birthmarks, which they called "witch-marks," as proof of a pact with the Devil. The court even accepted "spectral evidence," or claims of seeing the accused's spirit committing acts of malice, without question. The trials were often a farce, with the accused being forced to endure a series of humiliating and degrading rituals. Rituals that included being paraded through the streets, subjected to public shaming, and forced to confess to crimes they did not commit.

Torture was a common and cruel tool used to extract confessions. In Europe, inquisitors and witch-hunters used devices like the rack, thumb screws, and the notorious witch's chair to break the will of the accused. In Salem, though physical torture was less prevalent, psychological pressure was immense, with the accused being subjected to intense interrogation and intimidation.

In Salem, Giles Corey, an elderly man accused of witchcraft, was pressed to death with heavy stones after refusing to enter a plea. This is a stark example of the cruelty inflicted during these trials. Giles Corey's case was particularly horrifying. They subjected him to a brutal and inhumane form of torture known as "pressing," with heavy stones placed on his chest until he could not breathe. This form of torture was often used to extract confessions from the accused, and Corey's refusal to cooperate ultimately led to his death. The fact that Corey's case was so appalling highlights the extreme measures that were taken during the witch trials to extract confessions and maintain the illusion of justice.

Many of the executions were public affairs, intended to serve as both punishment and a deterrent. A sense of spectacle often accompanied the executions, with the townsfolk gathering to watch the accused meet their fate. In Europe, burning at the stake was the preferred method, a horrific spectacle that turned the accused into literal scapegoats for the community's fears. The burning of witches was often a public event. They would lead the accused to the stake in a procession, surrounded by cheering crowds and the sound of drums and trumpets. The execution itself was a gruesome affair, with the accused being tied to the stake and set ablaze. Their screams and pleas for mercy echoing through the air as they burned to death.

As the witch-hunts faded into history, people often forgot the lives of the executed. They buried many of them in unmarked graves, their names erased from collective memory. The erasure of their stories was possibly a deliberate attempt to erase the shame and guilt associated with the witch trials. But it also perpetuated the stigma and fear that had driven the accusations in the first place. Yet in recent decades, society has made efforts to reclaim their stories and honor their suffering.

The process of remembering has not been without challenges. In some cultures, the stigma associated with witchcraft persists, complicating efforts to reclaim the reputations of the accused. In some communities, the legacy of the witch trials continues to be felt, with people still whispering about the executed "witches." However, the growing recognition of the witch trials as a tragic chapter in human history has spurred greater interest in preserving the stories of the victims. Historians, researchers, and community leaders have worked tirelessly to uncover the stories of the accused, to document their lives and experiences, and to share their stories with the world.

In 1992, they established a memorial park in Salem, Massachusetts, to mark the 300th anniversary of the Salem Witch Trials. Designed by Maggie Smith and James Cutler, the memorial has 20 stone benches, each bearing the name of one of the executed victims alongside their execution date. The designers set the benches in a simple yet poignant layout within a walled area, symbolizing the accused's containment, isolation, and ostracization. The memorial also incorporates quotes from the condemned, such as "I am no witch," etched into the stone, a haunting reminder of their innocence.

The memorial park in Salem is just one example of the efforts being made to remember and honor the victims of the witch trials. Other communities around the world have also established memorials and museums to commemorate the lives of the accused. These efforts are not just about remembering the past, but also about acknowledging the harm that was done and the lives that were lost. By preserving the stories of the victims, we can understand the complexities of the witch trials and how fear, superstition, and prejudice can lead to tragedy. We can also heal the wounds of the past and work towards a more just and compassionate society.

Scotland experienced some of the most intense witch-hunting in Europe and has erected several memorials to commemorate the victims. Among the most prominent is the Witches' Well in Edinburgh, near Edinburgh Castle. They installed this small fountain and plaque in 1894 to commemorate the estimated 4,000 people, mostly women, executed for witchcraft in Scotland. Though modest in scale, the Witches' Well carries a powerful message about the human cost of superstition and fear.

There is a growing movement to create a national memorial for Scotland's accused witches. This movement aims to acknowledge the scale of the witch-hunts and create a comprehensive and respectful tribute to the persecuted.

One of the most striking and modern tributes to accused witches is the Steilneset Memorial in Vardø, Norway. This artistic installation, completed in 2011, commemorates the 91 people executed during the Finnmark Witch Trials in the 17th century. Designed by artist Louise Bourgeois and architect Peter Zumthor, the memorial features two structures. They comprise a long wooden corridor housing individual windows and plaques for each victim, and a glass cube containing a fiery installation symbolizing their suffering.

In Idstein, Germany, the Hexenturm, or "Witches' Tower," stands as both a historical site and a memorial. Originally used as a prison during the 17th-century witch trials, the tower now serves as a sobering reminder of the atrocities committed there. Exhibits within the tower recount the stories of the victims and the mechanisms of the trials, offering visitors a deeper understanding of the events. Its preservation underscores the importance of confronting and not replacing history to prevent similar injustices in the future.

Modern memorials to the victims of the witch trials serve as stark reminders of a dark period in human history. They are a way of honoring those who suffered unjustly while educating the public about the devastating consequences of fear, prejudice, and mass hysteria. These tributes take many forms, from physical monuments and museums to artistic works and community initiatives. Each one is a testament to the enduring power of remembrance and the importance of learning from the past. Preserving the stories of the accused and victims of the witch trials ensures we remember their struggles and sacrifices. We have a duty to preserve history's lessons for future generations.

Through these memorials, we strive to create a sense of empathy and understanding. We can once again humanize the victims of the witch trials and to challenge the simplistic narratives that often accompany this period in history. By confronting the complexities and nuances of the past, we can build a more compassionate and informed society, one that values justice, equality, and critical thinking over hysteria and scapegoating. Our reflection on the consequences of fear and prejudice reminds us to stand up against injustice. It also reminds us to advocate for the rights of the marginalized and promote a culture of tolerance and understanding.

In this way, modern memorials to the victims of the witch trials serve as a powerful tool for social change. They inspire us to create a brighter, more just future for all. By remembering the past, we can break free from the cycles of fear and hatred that have haunted human societies for centuries. Instead, we can forge a path towards a more enlightened, more compassionate world. Honoring the memories of those who suffered unjustly reminds us of the enduring power of the human spirit. And the importance of working towards a world where everyone can live with dignity, respect, and freedom.

CHAPTER 18
THE DECLINE OF WITCH-HUNTS

The early modern period, spanning roughly from the 15th to the 18th century, saw an unprecedented surge in witch-hunts across Europe and the Americas. At its peak, authorities accused, tried, and executed tens of thousands of individuals for alleged sorcery. Rooted in a blend of religious fervor, superstition, and social anxieties, the phenomenon represented one of history's darkest chapters. Yet, by the late 17th and early 18th centuries, the tide turned. Once fervently pursued as agents of evil, witches became the subject of skepticism, legal scrutiny, and even ridicule. The decline of witch-hunts marks a pivotal moment in the evolution of society, reflecting profound changes in legal, scientific, and religious thought.

Here, we will explore the complex web of factors that led to the decline of the witch-hunts. Learning how shifting legal frameworks, scientific advancements, and religious transformations underpinned this societal change. We'll investigate the role of Enlightenment thought, a key driver of the skepticism that ultimately dismantled widespread belief in witchcraft. Understanding the decline of witch-hunts provides insight into the interplay of fear, knowledge, and power, as well as the enduring capacity of societies to outgrow irrational and oppressive practices.

While the decline was neither uniform nor immediate, its trajectory reveals an unmistakable pattern as societies embraced reason and evidence over fear and superstition. By growing this way, the justification for witch trials crumbled. Let us trace this journey, unpacking the historical, cultural, and intellectual forces that converged to bring the end to centuries of witch-hunting.

Legal Reforms

One of the most significant factors contributing to the decline of witch-hunts was the transformation of legal systems across Europe. These changes reflected broader societal shifts toward rationality and fairness, limiting the ability of witchcraft accusations to thrive in judicial settings. The Enlightenment's emphasis on reason and individual rights eventually gained momentum. Opposite of the traditional inquisitorial approach to justice, which relied heavily on confessions gotten through torture and dubious testimony.

Legal reforms, including "habeas corpus" and the establishment of more stringent standards for gathering and presenting evidence, played pivotal roles in curbing the persecution of alleged witches. The gradual abandonment of torture, which had long been a cornerstone of the witch-hunting process, was a significant development. Authorities could no longer subject accused witches to gruesome physical coercion to extract confessions. This severely diminished the reliance on coerced testimony to establish guilt.

Moving to a higher standard of evidence, including the requirement of multiple eyewitness accounts and the prohibition on using hearsay as a basis for conviction, further eroded the witch-hunting apparatus. As a result, the number of executions for witchcraft declined. With this, the social and cultural stigma associated with witchcraft accusations gradually dissipated. The transformation of European legal systems marked a significant turning point in the history of witch-hunts. This paved the way for a more just and fair approach to justice and ultimately contributing to the decline of this dark chapter in human history.

During the height of the witch-hunts, courts often decided the outcome of accusations based on religious ideology or simple law rather than empirical evidence. However, by the 17th century, many governments and judicial bodies implemented reforms aimed at creating more rational and standardized legal systems.

In most witchcraft trials, investigators often extracted confessions under duress or torture. This frequently made the confession the basis of a guilty verdict. Using spectral evidence (testimony based on visions or dreams) also dominated proceedings, despite its inherently subjective and unverifiable nature. Over time, skepticism about these methods grew, prompting significant changes in legal procedure.

One of the critical developments was the growing centralization of judicial authority. Local or ecclesiastical courts, often swayed by community pressures and religious fervor, previously conducted many witch trials. As national governments merged power, they sought to impose stricter guidelines on legal proceedings. Centralized courts were less likely to validate accusations of witchcraft and more inclined to demand tangible evidence.

The gradual codification of laws also played a role in the decline. Legal systems such as England's Common Law required higher burdens of proof, making it increasingly difficult for witchcraft accusations to stand in court. For example, the 1736 Witchcraft Act in England marked a decisive break, effectively decriminalizing witchcraft and treating related accusations as fraudulent.

We know torture was a hallmark of the witch trials, which often lead to dramatic confessions. These confessions reinforced the belief in witches' existence. Instruments such as "thumbscrews", "racks", and "witches' chairs" were used to extract admissions of guilt, to break the accused's spirit and will to resist. These and other gruesome devices inflicted maximum pain and discomfort, intending to force the accused to confess to crimes they may not have committed. However, as legal systems further developed, the use of torture in judicial contexts became increasingly restricted, particularly in Western Europe.

Many legal thinkers criticized the reliance on torture, pointing out its unreliability in producing truthful confessions. They argued confessions gotten through coercion were inherently suspect and unreliable as evidence. The Roman Canon Law principle *Confessio extorta non valet* (a confession extracted by force is not valid) gained traction during this period. This law emphasized the importance of obtaining confessions through voluntary means. This principle formed a foundation of modern jurisprudence. For instance, in 1614, the *Constitutiones Criminales Carolinae* in the Holy Roman Empire emphasized procedural safeguards against the excessive use of torture. This marked a significant turning point in the decline of torture as a tool of interrogation.

In regions such as England and the Netherlands, torture was never formally enshrined as part of legal practice, even though commonly used by witch-hunters. However, this contributed to a more rapid decline in witch-hunts there, compared to countries like Germany or France. In England, authorities always considered torture a last resort, and even then, they subjected it to strict controls and oversight.

The Netherlands outright prohibited the use of torture, becoming a beacon of hope for those seeking refuge from the witch-hunts that ravaged other parts of Europe. Even in areas where torture persisted, the increasing scrutiny of its use led to gradual reductions in its application. As the tide of public opinion turned against torture, judges and magistrates questioned its use, and eventually, it fell out of favor to extract confessions.

Another major turning point in the decline of witch-hunts was the adoption of stricter evidentiary standards. Courts began to require concrete, verifiable proof rather than relying on hearsay, dreams, or confessions elicited under duress.

The Salem Witch Trials of 1692-1693 provide a striking example of the dangers posed by allowing spectral evidence. During the trials, accusations based on visions and dreams resulted in the execution of 20 individuals. However, public backlash and the intervention of figures like Increase Mather, who denounced spectral evidence in his essay *Cases of Conscience Concerning Evil Spirits*, helped to delegitimize its use.

Some courts now demanded material evidence of witchcraft, such as physical signs of a "witch's-mark" or the discovery of magickal tools. Over time, the inability to produce such evidence undermined many accusations. In addition, cross-examinations and testimonies from skeptics increasingly discredited accusers.

Scientific Advancements

The late Renaissance and Enlightenment periods saw significant advancements in the understanding of natural phenomena, from celestial mechanics to human biology. These developments undermined the belief in supernatural causes for misfortunes, such as crop failures, illnesses, or unexplainable deaths. This phenomenon was no longer being attributed to witches.

The early scientific thinkers challenged supernatural explanations for events such as storms, diseases, and miscarriages. For example, meteorological studies by scientists like Galileo Galilei and Evangelista Torricelli explained weather phenomena, reducing the inclination to blame witches for storms or droughts.

The medical field also advanced, offering natural explanations for conditions once seen as the result of curses or possession. Scientists increasingly studied mental illness, epilepsy, and other neurological disorders as medical conditions, rather than signs of demonic influence. Paracelsus, a 16th-century physician, was among the first to propose that such conditions had natural causes, paving the way for future medical inquiry.

Then the revolutionary work of Nicolaus Copernicus, Johannes Kepler, and Sir Isaac Newton reshaped humanity's understanding of the cosmos. The shift from a geocentric to a heliocentric model of the solar system and Newton's articulation of universal laws of motion and gravity diminished the mystical worldview. A view that had previously sustained the belief in witches as agents of cosmic chaos.

These are just a few of the scientific and intellectual figures that played a large role in challenging the belief in witchcraft. Their writings, lectures, and experiments exposed the irrationality of witch-hunts and offered new frameworks for understanding the natural world.

Historians often credit Francis Bacon with being the father of empiricism. Bacon promoted the use of inductive reasoning and systematic observation to uncover truths about the natural world. He argued that experience and observation, not authority or tradition, should provide the basis for knowledge. Bacon's rejection of superstition as an impediment to knowledge had a profound impact on the development of modern science. His approach influenced many subsequent thinkers to question the validity of supernatural explanations for natural phenomena. His emphasis on the importance of experimentation and the collection of data laid the foundation for the scientific method. An approach that would become the basis of scientific inquiry in the centuries to come.

Robert Boyle was a prominent chemist and physicist. Boyle's studies of gases and material properties reinforced a worldview based on natural laws rather than supernatural intervention. His groundbreaking work on the behavior of gases, which led to the development of the gas laws, demonstrated the predictability and regular arrangement of nature. Boyle's belief in the natural world as a rational and coherent system undermined the chaotic and unpredictable worldview that witchcraft theories relied upon. Boyle, by demonstrating that reason and observation, explained natural phenomena, contributed to increasing skepticism toward supernatural forces and the possibility of witchcraft.

Baruch Spinoza was a philosopher with a naturalistic view of the world. Spinoza contended that everything in existence is explainable through reason and natural laws. His writings rejected the idea of magick or supernatural forces, contributing to a broader skepticism about witchcraft. Spinoza's philosophy emphasized the importance of understanding the natural world through reason and observation, rather than relying on superstition or revelation. His ideas about the nature of God and the universe, an all-encompassing substance that underlies all of existence, further eroded the notion of supernatural intervention in the world.

Johann Weyer was a Dutch physician whose work predated the full flowering of the scientific revolution. However, his naturalistic explanations for alleged witchcraft, particularly his view that many accused witches suffered from psychological disorders, laid important groundwork for scientific skepticism. Weyer's book, *De Praestigiis Daemonum (On the Deception of Demons)*, challenged the traditional view of witchcraft as a supernatural phenomenon. Instead, his work attributed many alleged cases of witchcraft to mental illness, superstition, or deception. His work marked a significant turning point in the development of modern skepticism about witchcraft. He paved the way for later thinkers to question the validity of witchcraft theories and the use of torture and other forms of coercion to extract confessions.

As these scientific methodologies gained prominence, the reliance on anecdotal or unverified claims diminished. Empirical evidence, rooted in observation and experimentation, replaced superstition and hearsay as the standard for truth.

It became standard practice for early scientists to conduct experiments to test theories about the physical world, challenging the validity of claims rooted in superstition. For example, William Harvey's experiments on blood circulation showed that biology, not mystical forces, could explain life processes.

This was the scientific revolution which led to the rise of scientific societies. Institutions such as the Royal Society, founded in 1660, became centers of intellectual exchange, promoting the application of reason and the scientific method. These societies often hosted debates about witchcraft, with many members expressing skepticism about the supernatural. This scientific approach influenced legal and societal standards for evidence. The dismissal of unsubstantiated claims increased, making it harder to sustain accusations of witchcraft.

The scientific revolution fundamentally altered humanity's understanding of cause and effect. As the belief in supernatural causation faded, so too did the rationale for witch-hunts. Natural processes increasingly explained events such as plagues, crop failures, and accidents previously attributed to witches. For example, advances in agricultural science reduced the association between poor harvests and witchcraft.

Critics increasingly dismissed or criticized demonological texts, such as Heinrich Kramer's *Malleus Maleficarum*, which had fueled the witch-hunts, as unscientific. The rational worldview that emerged from the scientific revolution left little room for belief in demons or their supposed agents.

However, there remained a tension between religious order, scientific thought and a superstitious communal belief in witchcraft until the late 1800s. Sometimes, religious authorities resisted the spread of scientific ideas, viewing them as threats to established doctrine. This tension slowed the decline of witch-hunts in regions where religious orthodoxy remained strong. While among rural populations, where education and scientific knowledge were less accessible, belief in witchcraft remained common. However, even in these areas, the influence of scientific thought gradually seeped in, eroding traditional superstitions.

This shift from a supernatural to a naturalistic worldview extended beyond the issue of witchcraft. This new way of thinking influenced nearly every aspect of society. The intellectual climate fostered by the scientific revolution prepared the grounds for the Enlightenment, which would further challenge the belief in witches.

The application of reason and empirical evidence to human affairs helped lay the foundations for modern concepts of justice and individual rights. Both of which opposed the arbitrary and oppressive nature of the witch trials.

As the scientific revolution gained momentum, thinkers questioned the notion that dubious accusations and unproven claims could justify torturing, imprisoning, and executing individuals. The emphasis on reason, evidence, and empirical observation provided a powerful counterweight to the superstition and prejudice that had fueled the witch-hunts. By emphasizing the importance of individual rights and protecting the innocent, the scientific revolution helped to establish a more just and fair society. A society where the rule of law and the principles of due process became paramount.

The principles of rationality and evidence-based inquiry that emerged from the scientific revolution provided the intellectual tools necessary to dismantle other forms of persecution rooted in superstition or prejudice. As the scientific method became more widely accepted, thinkers applied its principles to a broader range of social and political issues.

The emphasis on reason, observation, and experimentation helped to challenge traditional authority and superstition. This paved the way for a more rational and enlightened approach to governance. By applying the principles of science to human affairs, thinkers could develop a more nuanced understanding of the world and its complexities, leading to a more just and fair society. The scientific revolution's emphasis on individual rights, due process, and protecting the innocent helped to establish a more rational framework for society. One that prioritized the well-being and dignity of all individuals.

Religious Transformation

Religious changes during the early modern period were another critical factor in the decline of witch-hunts. While religion had initially fueled the fear of witches through its emphasis on the Devil and heresy, it eventually became a force for moderation and skepticism. The Reformation and Counter-Reformation, shifts in theological interpretations, and the growing separation between superstition and institutional religion eventually contributed to diminishing the zeal for witch-hunts.

The Protestant Reformation (1517–1648) and the Catholic Counter-Reformation (1545–1648) reshaped the religious landscape of Europe. By each trying to gain control, they altered attitudes toward witchcraft in both subtle and profound ways. The Protestant Reformation, led by figures such as Martin Luther and John Calvin, challenged the authority of the

Catholic Church. They introduced new ideas about God, salvation, and the role of the individual in the spiritual realm. History proves the early years of the Reformation saw an increase in witch-hunts, particularly in areas where Protestantism was gaining traction as both sides fought to gain followers.

The Protestant Reformation's rejection of Catholic doctrine and tradition helped to undermine the cultural and social context that had fueled the witch-hunts. As Protestantism spread, the notion of witchcraft as a supernatural threat to the community lost its hold. This shifted the focus from the persecution of witches to the persecution of heretics and non-conformists. The Catholic Counter-Reformation sought to counter the spread of Protestantism and restore the authority of the Catholic Church. While the Counter-Reformation initially intensified witch-hunts in some areas, particularly in regions where Catholicism was under threat, it ultimately contributed to a more rational and evidence-based approach to witchcraft.

After the Peace of Westphalia and the Thirty Years' War, both the Protestant Reformation and the Catholic Counter-Reformation had helped to curtail the witch-hunts that had ravaged Europe for centuries. Protestantism's emphasis on individualism, personal faith, and the authority of scripture combined with the Catholic Church's efforts to reform and rationalize its approach to witchcraft, helped create a more nuanced understanding of the phenomenon. As the scientific revolution gained momentum, thinkers questioned the notion of witchcraft as a supernatural threat, and the witch-hunts that had characterized the early modern period faded into memory.

Early Protestant reformers like Martin Luther and John Calvin reinforced a belief in the Devil's active role in the world, which validated the fear of witches. In some Protestant regions, the drive to eradicate heresy extended to rooting out witchcraft. For example, Protestant territories in Germany witnessed some of the most intense witch-hunts during the 16th and 17th centuries.

The Catholic Church, in its effort to reassert authority during the Counter-Reformation, also intensified witch-hunts in certain regions. The Spanish Inquisition, while often more concerned with heresy than witchcraft, contributed to the atmosphere of suspicion and persecution.

Over time, both Protestant and Catholic authorities changed their views on witchcraft. By the mid-17th century, prominent clergy in both traditions questioned the validity of witch trials. For example, Friedrich Spee, a Jesuit priest, denounced the persecution of witches in his 1631 book *Cautio Criminalis*. In it, he argued the accused were often innocent victims of hysteria and false accusations.

As theological thought evolved, the belief in witches and their supposed powers became increasingly marginalized within religious discourse. Earlier religious views depicted the Devil as an omnipresent force actively corrupting humanity. This belief justified the notion that witches were his agents. By the late 17th century, however, theologians adopted a more restrained view of his power. They argued that God's omnipotence rendered the Devil's influence minimal, undermining the notion that witches could wield such supernatural power.

Both Protestant and Catholic movements learned to emphasize personal faith and morality over external threats, like witchcraft. This inward turn made accusations of witchcraft seem increasingly irrelevant to religious practice. Religious leaders distinguished between genuine religious belief and superstition. Religious leaders increasingly categorized witchcraft, with its reliance on charms, spells, and rituals, as superstition rather than legitimate theology. This shift further distanced mainstream religion from the fear of witches.

One of the most significant changes in this period was the growing divide between institutional religion and folk superstitions. Whereas earlier Christian leaders had often endorsed popular beliefs in witches and magick, later religious authorities sought to discredit and suppress such practices.

By the 18th century, many clergy members dismissed belief in witchcraft as incompatible with enlightened religious thought. For instance, the Anglican Bishop Francis Hutchinson wrote *An Historical Essay Concerning Witchcraft* (1718), which criticized witch trials and highlighted the lack of evidence for supernatural activity.

As Christianity continued to develop, both Protestant and Catholic authorities began a concerted effort to dissociate their faith from magickal practices. This process of "purification" entailed the condemnation of superstitions that had previously contributed to the proliferation of witch-hunts. By considering these practices as remnants of paganism, Christian theologians sought to establish a clearer distinction between their faith and the occult. This development marked a significant shift in the theological landscape, as the Church distanced itself from the very superstitions that had once fueled the persecution of the alleged witches.

The rise of religious tolerance in Europe during the Enlightenment also contributed to the decline of witch-hunts. As societies moved toward greater acceptance of diverse religious practices, the persecution of individuals for their beliefs or actions became less justifiable.

In some regions, the interfaith dialogue between Catholics and Protestants fostered an atmosphere of mutual understanding. This shift reduced the ideological tensions that had previously driven witch-hunts.

The growing separation between church and state also diminished the role of religion in legal matters. Secular courts, less influenced by theological concerns, were more likely to dismiss witchcraft accusations as baseless.

Throughout the decline of the witch-hunts, certain religious leaders emerged as outspoken critics of the practice, using their authority to challenge prevailing beliefs. The Salem Witch Trials of 1692-1693 provide a poignant example of religious leaders' shifting attitudes. While figures like Reverend Samuel Parris initially fueled the hysteria, others, such as Increase Mather, later condemned the trials, emphasizing the need for evidence and rationality. Even within devout religious circles, figures like John Wesley of the Methodist movement questioned the legitimacy of witchcraft accusations. Wesley's writings often emphasized personal salvation and spiritual growth over the persecution of supposed witches.

Religious transformations played a dual role in the decline of witch-hunts. While earlier periods of religious upheaval intensified fears of witchcraft, the eventual moderation of theological views and the growing distinction between religion and superstition laid the groundwork for skepticism. The emergence of religious tolerance and the influence of critical clergy further accelerated this process, making the persecution of witches incompatible with the changing values of early modern societies.

. . .

Enlightenment Thought

We cannot fully understand the decline in witch-hunts without considering the broader religious context of skepticism that developed during the Enlightenment. The Enlightenment was a transformative period in Western history, which brought about a profound shift in the intellectual and cultural landscape of the time. Emerging in the late 17th century and flourishing in the 18th, the Enlightenment ushered in an era of critical inquiry, skepticism, and rationalism. This directly challenged the foundations of a belief in witchcraft. The growing emphasis on evidence, reason, and human rights characterized this intellectual movement, often called the "Age of Reason." An age that collectively contributed to the erosion of superstitions and the decline of witch-hunts.

In the heart of the Enlightenment lay a commitment to critical thinking and empirical evidence. Philosophers, scientists, and writers of this period challenged traditional authority and dogma. They instead advocated for a more nuanced understanding of the world based on observation, experimentation, and logical reasoning. The works of prominent Enlightenment thinkers, such as René Descartes, John Locke, and Immanuel Kant, who developed philosophical frameworks that prioritized reason and individualism exemplified this approach. The writings of these thinkers, among others, helped to spread Enlightenment ideas and values, gradually shaping the intellectual climate of the time.

The Enlightenment's impact on the decline of witch-hunts was multifaceted. By emphasizing the importance of evidence and reason, Enlightenment thinkers undermined the legitimacy of witchcraft accusations, which had long relied on hearsay, superstition, and unverifiable testimony. The growing recognition of human rights and the inherent value of human life also contributed to a shift in societal attitudes. People viewed witch-hunts as more a form of persecution rather than a necessary measure of protecting society. The Enlightenment's emphasis on individualism and personal autonomy undermined the concept of collective guilt and the idea of holding individuals responsible for others' actions.

Because of these intellectual and cultural developments, the intellectual climate of the Enlightenment played a pivotal role in the decline of witch-hunts. Reason, evidence, and human rights, emphasized during this period, fostered a society increasingly skeptical of witchcraft accusations.

Central to the Enlightenment was the rejection of unverified beliefs and traditions, including witchcraft. Enlightenment thinkers examined the social and intellectual frameworks that supported the persecution of witches, exposing their irrationality and injustice.

Philosophers like Voltaire, David Hume, and Montesquieu criticized the belief in witchcraft as a product of ignorance and fear. Voltaire, for example, denounced witch trials as cruel and baseless in his writings. He famously remarked in the *Philosophical Dictionary* that "those who can make you believe absurdities can make you commit atrocities."

Philosophers like Thomas Hobbes and John Locke brought empirical reasoning to bear on the question of witchcraft. Hobbes, in *Leviathan* (1651), argued that belief in witches stemmed from psychological manipulation and irrational fears, rather than any real supernatural phenomena. Locke's emphasis on evidence-based inquiry further discredited unscientific claims about witchcraft.

Enlightenment thought emphasized a secular moral fabric that valued justice and individual rights over religious dogma. Witch-hunts, which often relied on vague accusations and brutal punishments, became increasingly incompatible with these emerging ethical standards.

The Enlightenment's emphasis on individual rights, legal reform, and skepticism of authority had a profound impact on the practice of witch-hunts. Philosophers and legal reformers played a crucial role in exposing the injustices of witch trials, advocating for procedural fairness and the rejection of supernatural explanations in legal proceedings.

One of the key critiques of the Enlightenment was the arbitrary use of power, particularly by religious and judicial authorities. Witch-hunts, which often involved the use of torture, arbitrary confessions, and unfair trials, became emblematic of the abuses that Enlightenment thinkers sought to rectify. The Enlightenment's emphasis on the rule of law, due process, and protecting individual rights helped to challenge the legitimacy of witch trials and the authority of those who conducted them.

The work of Cesare Beccaria was instrumental in reforming European legal practices. His treatise, *On Crimes and Punishments* (1764), argued against the use of torture and emphasized the importance of evidence in legal proceedings. Beccaria's ideas helped to undermine the foundation of witch trials, which had long relied on dubious evidence and supernatural explanations. By promoting a more rational and evidence-based approach to justice, Beccaria's work contributed to a shift away from the arbitrary and oppressive practices.

The Enlightenment's emphasis on public debate and critical thinking also helped to shift public opinion on witch-hunts. Exonerations in high-profile cases of accused witches illustrated the dangers of irrational legal practices, while Enlightenment-era publications brought these issues of injustice to the forefront. As a result, skepticism toward witch-hunts grew, and the practice of witch trials declined.

Enlightenment thinkers rejected supernatural explanations for natural phenomena and instead sought logical and observable causes. The shift in perspective made witchcraft accusations increasingly implausible. Reason now explained misfortunes like plagues and crop failures.

Philosophers such as Immanuel Kant argued for the use of reason as the ultimate tool for understanding the world. Kant's *What Is Enlightenment?* (1784) called for intellectual freedom and the courage to think independently, which directly opposed the blind acceptance of witchcraft allegations. Pierre Bayle criticized the irrationality of witch trials in works such as *Dictionnaire Historique et Critique* (1697), where he meticulously dissected the errors and fallacies in popular beliefs about witches.

The proliferation of books, pamphlets, and newspapers during the Enlightenment period facilitated the widespread dissemination of critical ideas, including those that challenged the notion of witchcraft. Writers and intellectuals employed satire as a powerful tool to ridicule the superstitions surrounding witchcraft, framing it as a relic of a bygone era. For instance, in England, satirical plays and essays effectively mocked the absurdity of witch trials, eroding public support for such practices.

The Enlightenment's emphasis on public discourse and debate also played a significant role in shaping attitudes toward witchcraft. Salons, coffeehouses, and lecture halls served as forums for intellectuals and ordinary citizens to engage in discussions on contemporary issues, including witchcraft. These debates fostered critical thinking and challenged long-held superstitions, contributing to a more nuanced understanding of the world.

The Enlightenment's emphasis on education also had a profound impact. As literacy rates increased and schools incorporated scientific and philosophical ideas, younger generations became less likely to accept the supernatural explanations that had sustained witch-hunts. The dissemination of Enlightenment ideas through education helped to create a more rational and informed public.

Thinkers like Voltaire and Beccaria argued passionately against the use of torture and the death penalty, practices originally central to the persecution of witches. Their arguments influenced legal reforms across Europe. While the Enlightenment did not fully address gender inequality, its principles of universal human rights contributed to a gradual reassessment of the role of women in society. Given that most accused witches were women, this reevaluation played a role in curbing the practice.

The Enlightenment's impact on witchcraft beliefs was not instantaneous, and remnants of superstition persisted in many areas, some to this day. However, its intellectual currents created a lasting legacy that ultimately rendered witch-hunts obsolete.

In some rural regions, where Enlightenment ideas were slow to penetrate, belief in witches and occasional trials persisted into the 18th century. However, newer modern values increasingly deemed these occurrences backward and out of step.

The Enlightenment was a transformative period that dismantled the intellectual foundations of witch-hunts. By emphasizing reason, evidence, and human rights, Enlightenment thinkers exposed the irrationality and injustice of witch trials, contributing to their decline. While remnants of superstition persisted, the legacy of the Enlightenment ensured that belief in witchcraft would never regain its former dominance.

CHAPTER 19
LEGACY OF WITCH-HUNTERS AND THE HUNTED

The history of the witch-hunters is a dark and foreboding chapter in humanity's past, marked by fear, bloodshed, and a profound disregard for human life. It was a time when paranoia and superstition ran rampant. When the belief in unseen forces and supernatural powers shaped laws, governance, and social interactions in ways that are as fascinating as they are terrifying. The witch-hunters were often driven by a zealous desire to root out evil and maintain control. They wielded authority with an iron fist, leaving a trail of destruction and despair in their wake.

But the witch-hunting craze was never merely just about a belief in magick or the supernatural. It was about power, control, and a desperate attempt to explain what was then unexplainable. In a world where the unknown was a constant threat, the witch-hunters saw themselves as the guardians of order and morality. Tasked with protecting society from the perceived evil that lurked in every shadow. And yet, as we now know, their methods were often brutal and unjust. They relied heavily on dubious evidence, coerced confessions, and a willingness to believe the worst about their fellow human beings.

From the witch-hunters who orchestrated the trials to the hunted, the accusations shattered their lives and left an indelible mark on history. The witch-hunters were often driven by a sense of righteousness and a desire for power. They manipulated a fragile system to their advantage. Many used their positions of authority to silence their critics and eliminate their enemies. They subjected the accused to unimaginable suffering while the accusations forever tarnished their reputations and the stigma of being labeled a witch tore their lives apart.

Even today, centuries later, the echoes of the witch-hunts persist. Not only in historical records but also in our cultural memory, laws, and societal attitudes. The legacy of the witch trials continues to influence modern discussions about justice, fear, and power dynamics, serving as a cautionary tale.

As we now know, witch-hunting was not a singular event confined to one nation or culture. It is a widespread phenomenon that spans continents and centuries. Between the 15th and 18th centuries, Europe and its colonies saw a surge in witch trials, resulting in the persecution and execution of tens of thousands. A confluence of religious fervor, political instability, and social upheaval fueled the infamous European witch craze.

The history of witch-hunting is full of key moments that highlight the depths of human depravity. One of the most infamous texts to emerge from this era is the *Malleus Maleficarum* (*The Hammer of Witches*), published in 1487 by Heinrich Kramer and Jacob Sprenger. This theological and legal treatise provided a justification for witch-hunting that was both comprehensive and chilling. It served as a foundational manual for inquisitors and secular authorities alike. The *Malleus Maleficarum* was a masterclass in how to blur the lines between superstition and governance. It treated the crime of witchcraft as an existential threat to society that required the most extreme measures to eradicate.

Their reliance on dubious evidence and their willingness to sacrifice due process in the name of rooting out evil often characterized the witch-hunting manuals of this era. These texts provided the framework for inquisitors and authorities to extract confessions from accused witches using torture and other forms of coercion. Ultimately, they legitimized the use of hearsay and spectral sightings as evidence. The result was a system of justice that was often little more than a sham, with accused witches facing trial and execution based on flimsy evidence and personal vendettas.

The Salem Witch Trials of 1692 in colonial America stand as a stark example of how fear and mass hysteria can devastate a community. Over a few short months, the executions of twenty people and the accusations of witchcraft against hundreds more resulted from using the same questionable evidence employed in Europe for centuries. The trials were a mixture of paranoia, superstition, and poor governance. They subjected the accused to phycological torture and other forms of coercion in order to extract confessions, and the trials themselves were not fair or just.

As the witch craze waned in the 18th century, Enlightenment ideals and advances in science began to undermine the belief in witchcraft and the supernatural. The rise of rationalism and empiricism provided a new understanding of the world. An understanding that emphasized the importance of evidence and observation over superstition and hearsay. However, they could not easily erase the societal scars left by centuries of persecution. The legacy of the witch trials continues to influence modern discussions about justice, fear, and power dynamics.

Survivors of the witch trials endured profound and multifaceted suffering that went far beyond the courtroom and execution grounds. For those who escaped execution, life was often a shadow of what it had once been. The stigma of being accused as a witch marked individuals, families, and entire communities, leaving deep psychological and social scars that persisted for generations. While the stories of those who perished dominate the historical narrative, the experiences of survivors and their descendants shed light on the far-reaching consequences of these persecutions.

A profound and lasting impact on the lives of survivors marked the aftermath of the trials. While they evaded the ultimate penalty of death, the social, economic, and psychological consequences of being accused of witchcraft were severe and far-reaching. Being labeled a witch led to social ostracism, as friends, neighbors, and even family members distanced themselves from the accused. They distanced themselves either out of fear of association or because they believed the accusations. This social isolation cruelly forced survivors to navigate a world where they were no longer included in their former communities.

The economic consequences of witchcraft accusations were equally devastating. Many times, confiscation of property by authorities accompanied the accusation, leaving individuals and families destitute. This financial ruin was particularly pronounced among women, who were already economically vulnerable in patriarchal societies. A widow accused of witchcraft, for example, might lose her home and any inheritance, leaving her unable to provide for herself or her children.

Beyond the social and economic consequences, survivors of witch trials also suffered severe physical and emotional trauma. Torture was a common practice during interrogations, often leaving those who survived with permanent injuries. The psychological toll of these experiences, along with fear, humiliation, and betrayal, would haunt survivors for the rest of their lives. The trauma of witchcraft accusations inflicts psychological violence, affecting mental health and well-being long-term. We should consider the experience of being a witch trial survivor a form of social death, stripping the individual of social status, economic security, and even self-worth.

The Pendle Witch Trials of 1612 illustrate the profound suffering of survivors. Of the twelve accused townsfolk, only Alice Grey received an acquittal. Though she escaped execution, the ordeal irrevocably altered Alice's life. Records suggest the trials tarnished her reputation and limited her ability to reintegrate into society. The stigma of the accusation undermined the community's willingness to accept her as an innocent woman. Townsfolk often viewed survivors like Alice with suspicion, as if their escape from execution proved supernatural intervention.

The trauma of witchcraft accusations extended beyond the individual victims by deeply affecting their families. Being related to an accused witch often meant inheriting the perceived disgrace. The communities frequently ostracized, bullied, or abandoned the children of the accused, considering them tainted by association. This social exclusion could make it nearly impossible for descendants to marry, secure employment, or live free from suspicion.

For many families, the trauma of a witch accusation became a story that was silenced or suppressed. Many descendants deliberately avoided discussing their ancestors to escape the shadow of the past. This suppression of family history is itself a form of generational trauma, as the pain and injustice endured by ancestors remain unresolved and unacknowledged.

The Salem Witch Trials of 1692 provide a stark and well-documented example of the long-lasting impact of this type of generational trauma. The families of the accused and executed faced economic and social repercussions that lasted for decades, leaving a lasting scar on their descendants. Elizabeth Proctor, for instance, was a victim of the trials who survived, but only after being convicted of witchcraft and imprisoned while pregnant. John Proctor, her husband, suffered the misfortune of hanging in 1692. This left their children, John Jr. and Mercy, to rebuild their lives in a community that continued to view their family name with suspicion and distrust.

The Proctor family experienced trauma that extended beyond the immediate aftermath of the trials. For generations, the accusations of witchcraft tarnished the family's reputation, and they faced social and economic ostracism. Authorities confiscated the family's property, forcing them to live in poverty. John and Elizabeth Proctor's children grew up in a world where their family's name was synonymous with witchcraft, and they struggled to overcome the stigma attached to them.

Despite the challenges they faced, the descendants of the Proctors have worked to reclaim their family history, turning it into a narrative of resilience and survival. In recent years, there has been a growing interest in the Proctor family's story, and many have sought to learn more about their ancestors and the experiences they endured. This renewed interest has allowed the

Proctor family to begin the process of healing and reconciliation and to reclaim their place in American history. By sharing their story, the Proctors have been able to break free from the stigma of witchcraft. Allowing them to forge a new identity that is based on their strength and resilience in the face of adversity.

By using modern research, we can begin to understand the psychological impact of witch-hunting on the survivors and their descendants. Survivors often displayed symptoms we would now recognize as post-traumatic stress disorder (PTSD): anxiety, depression, hypervigilance, and difficulty trusting others. Their experiences shaped how they interacted with the world, often leading to a life marked by fear and isolation.

Generational trauma refers to the transmission of trauma's effects from one generation to the next. Studies on descendants of marginalized or persecuted groups, such as Holocaust survivors or indigenous communities affected by colonization, reveal patterns of inherited fear, shame, and resilience. With the witch trials, the stigma attached to accused families likely influenced how descendants perceived themselves and interacted with their communities. This legacy of trauma could manifest in silence, a reluctance to trust authority, or a deep-seated need to defend one's reputation.

This impact extended beyond individual families to entire communities. The culture of accusation and betrayal during the witch craze often destroyed the social fabric of small villages and towns. A legacy of mistrust in communities where witch trials occurred resulted from this. Communal trauma took generations to heal, particularly in regions where the trials claimed many lives. The mass trials in Bamberg and Würzburg, Germany, for example, deeply scarred the population after executing hundreds. Churches and local authorities that had once served as sources of moral and social guidance were now seen as accomplices to the injustice.

The systems of control established during the witch craze did not disappear with the trials. They evolved and adapted into new contexts. The inquisitorial methods used in the witch trials relied on anonymous accusations, coercive interrogations, and public punishments, becoming templates for other forms of state persecution. This period refined and perfected these methods, which were not unique to witch trials, creating a model for future repression.

The reliance on anonymous accusations, for example, allowed the state to target individuals without having to provide any evidence or justification. This created a culture of fear and mistrust, where people were afraid to speak out against the authorities or to question the accusations made against them. Using coercive interrogations, including torture and other forms of physical and psychological abuse, was also a hallmark of the witch trials. This power dynamic left the accused at the mercy of their interrogators, who often forced confessions to crimes they did not commit.

Using public punishments, such as executions and burnings at the stake, was also a key feature of the witch trials. These public spectacles reinforced the power of the state and it intimidated potential dissenters. They also created a sense of community and shared values, as people came together to witness the punishment of those deemed to be enemies of the state. Similar techniques used in other forms of state persecution, including the Spanish Inquisition, McCarthyism of the 1950s, and modern-day torture and rendition, demonstrate the legacy of these inquisitorial methods.

The evolution of these systems of control is a testament to the enduring power of the state to shape and manipulate the behavior of its citizens. The witch trials may have been a product of a specific historical moment, but the methods used during that time have had a lasting impact. It exemplifies how states interacted with their citizens. By understanding the history of the witch trials and the systems of control that were established during that time, we can gain a deeper knowledge. A knowledge of how the state has shaped our world and continues to shape our lives.

CHAPTER 20
LESSONS FROM WITCH HUNTS FOR TODAY'S WORLD

The witch-hunts of the early modern period left an indelible mark on history, influencing the way societies interpret fear, justice, and persecution. Though the era of widespread trials and executions eventually ended, the legacy of these events continues to resonate in various aspects of modern culture, law, and thought. The witch-hunts serve as a poignant reminder of the dangers of unchecked fear, the importance of protecting individual rights, and the need for critical thinking in the face of uncertainty.

As the years have passed, historians, scholars, and the public have reinterpreted and reevaluated the witch-hunts. Initially, society often viewed the trials as a necessary evil, a means of protecting communities and townsfolk from the perceived threat of witchcraft and the Devil. However, as the 20th century progressed, a more nuanced understanding of the witch-hunts emerged. Historians examined the social, cultural, and economic contexts in which the trials took place, revealing the complex web of factors that contributed to them. This new perspective has led to a greater recognition of the witch-hunts as a manifestation of societal fears, superstitions, and power struggles.

We can see the legacy of the witch-hunts in various aspects of modern culture, law, and thought. In the realm of law, they serve as a cautionary tale about the dangers of arbitrary power and the importance of protecting individual rights. The trials also highlight the need for due process and the importance of evidence-based decision-making. In modern culture, the witch-hunts have inspired many works of literature, art, and film, serving as a reminder of the darker aspects of human nature. They have influenced the way we think about fear, superstition, and the unknown, encouraging us to approach these topics with a critical and nuanced perspective.

The lessons of that horrible period are multifaceted and far-reaching. They remind us of the importance of protecting individual rights and the need for critical thinking in the face of uncertainty. The trials also highlight the dangers of unchecked power, fear and the importance of addressing social fears and superstitions in a constructive and rational manner. Ultimately, the witch-hunts offer a powerful reminder of the importance of empathy, compassion. Providing us an understanding of our interactions with others, and the need to approach complex issues with a nuanced and informed perspective.

We have remembered and reinterpreted the witch-hunting craze of the early modern period in various ways, reflecting changing attitudes and cultural values. These interpretations provide insight into the enduring impact of these historical events on modern society, as well as how they continue to influence our understanding of fear, power, and injustice.

People remember them significantly as a symbol of irrational and unjust persecution. The term "witch-hunt" has become a metaphor for baseless accusations, moral panics, and the arbitrary exercise of power. This association reflects the widespread recognition of the witch-hunt phenomenon as a cautionary tale about the dangers of unchecked power, fear, hysteria, and the erosion of due process.

They have also inspired a vast array of artistic representations, from literature to theater and visual art. These works often reinterpret the events to explore themes of fear, power, and societal breakdown, highlighting the complexities and nuances of these historical events. For example, Arthur Miller's play *The Crucible* (1953) uses the Salem Witch Trials as an allegory for McCarthyism, underscoring the dangers of mass hysteria and political scapegoating.

The history of the witch-hunters and the hunted offer a rich and complex case study for understanding the dynamics of fear, power, and justice in society. These events provide valuable lessons that remain relevant in addressing modern forms of persecution and mass hysteria.

One of the most significant lessons from them is the danger of moral panics, where fear and superstition can escalate into irrational and destructive behavior. The witch-hunts show how societies can become gripped by mass hysteria, leading to the erosion of rationality and the disregard for due process. We can observe this phenomenon in more recent events, such as the Satanic Panic of the 1980s and 1990s. A modern time where false accusations of ritual abuse led to widespread fear and wrongful convictions. Understanding the dynamics of moral panics is essential for preventing similar events from occurring in the future.

The witch-hunts also highlight the role of scapegoating in times of crisis. Societies often target marginalized groups as scapegoats, perpetuating patterns of social inequality and oppression. The witch-hunts exemplified this tendency, with women, the elderly, and the poor being disproportionately accused of witchcraft. Recognizing this pattern is crucial for preventing similar forms of discrimination in the future.

The trials also underscored the importance of due process and fair legal procedures. The arbitrary and unjust nature of the witch trials highlights the need for legal systems that prioritize justice and human rights. A lack of evidence, reliance on torture, and absence of proper defense during the trials show the importance of protecting individual rights.

Although people often view witch-hunts as a phenomenon of the past, we can still observe their underlying dynamics in contemporary society. These parallels serve as a warning about the persistence of irrational fears and the human capacity for persecution.

We often describe the anti-communist fervor of the 1950s in the United States, spearheaded by Senator Joseph McCarthy, as a "witch-hunt" because of its reliance on baseless accusations and fearmongering. Like the witch-hunts of the early modern period, McCarthyism targeted individuals based on suspicion rather than evidence, leading to ruined lives and careers. The parallels between the two phenomena are striking with unchecked power, mass hysteria, and the erosion of due process.

During the height of McCarthyism, a climate of fear and paranoia gripped the United States, fueled by the Cold War and the perceived threat of communism. Senator McCarthy, with his mob leading rhetoric and sensationalist tactics, exploited this crusade against alleged communists and "fellow travelers" in government, entertainment, and academia. McCarthy often based his accusations on flimsy evidence, hearsay, or mere suspicion, and frequently subjected the accused to public humiliation, blacklisting, and even imprisonment.

The consequences of McCarthyism were devastating, with countless lives, and careers ruined by the unfounded accusations. The House Un-American Activities Committee (HUAC), established in 1938, was instrumental in perpetuating this witch-hunt, using its subpoena power to compel witnesses to testify against their colleagues and friends. The Red Scare, as it became known, fostered a climate of terror, where the fear of being accused of communism or treason silenced dissenting voices.

During the late 20th century, allegations of satanic ritual abuse swept through parts of the United States and other countries, echoing the dynamics of earlier witch-hunts. These accusations were often based on questionable testimony, hearsay, and unverified claims, leading to a wave of moral panic that would ultimately result in the wrongful conviction of many individuals. The Satanic Panic, as it came to be known, was a stark reminder of the enduring potential for moral panics to harm innocent people. It provides another example of the importance of protecting due process and individual rights.

This particular Satanic Panic began in the 1980s, with reports of satanic ritual abuse emerging in various parts of the United States. Sensationalized media coverage and the testimony of self-proclaimed experts. These experts claimed to have uncovered evidence of widespread satanic activity, which often fueled these allegations. However, as investigations into these claims progressed, it became clear that many of the allegations were based on dubious evidence and hearsay. Despite this, the moral panic surrounding satanic ritual abuse continued to grow, with many individuals being accused and convicted of crimes they did not commit.

The Satanic Panic led to the wrongful conviction of parents, caregivers, teachers, and even children. Investigators subjected many of these individuals to coercive interrogation techniques, including hypnosis and other forms of psychological manipulation. The consequences of these convictions were devastating, with many individuals losing their freedom, their families, and their reputations. The Satanic Panic also led to the establishment of so called "treatment centers" and "recovery programs" that promised to help individuals overcome the supposed trauma of satanic ritual abuse. However, many of these programs were little more than pseudoscientific scams, designed to extract money from vulnerable individuals and families.

In the age of social media, online "witch-hunts" have emerged as a modern form of public shaming. It provides an outlet where accusations, whether or not grounded in fact, spread rapidly online. This has led to reputational damage and even threats of violence. This phenomenon reflects the same dynamics of fear, scapegoating, and mob mentality that characterized the historical witch-hunts. The ease of online information sharing and dissemination creates a perfect situation for the rapid spread of misinformation and public shaming of individuals.

The rapid mobilization of online mobs can characterize the digital age witch-hunt phenomenon. These mobs often rely on social media platforms to spread accusations and condemn individuals without due process or evidence. This can lead to public shaming, ostracization, and even threats of violence against individuals before any formal investigation or trial. The consequences of digital age witch-hunts can be severe, with individuals losing their jobs, their reputations, and even their life.

The dynamics of digital age witch-hunts are eerily similar to those of historical witch-hunts. In both cases, fear, superstition, and mob mentality play a significant role in the targeting and persecution of individuals. The ease of online information sharing allows accusations to spread rapidly, often disregarding evidence or due process. This has created a situation where accusations often condemn and shame individuals before any formal investigation, denying the accused a chance to defend themselves.

The digital age witch-hunt phenomenon also highlights the need for greater awareness and understanding of the dangers of online mob mentality and the erosion of due process. By examining this phenomenon, we can gain a deeper understanding of how social media can spread misinformation and target individuals for public shaming. We can also learn from the lessons of history and work towards creating a more just and fair society. We can do this by protecting individuals from the dangers of mob mentality and upholding due process.

Using a feminist lens, scholars have extensively studied the early modern period's witch-hunts, highlighting the disproportionate targeting of women and the reinforcement of patriarchal power structures. Research suggests that approximately 75-80% of those accused of witchcraft during this period were women, often characterized by their marital status, socioeconomic position, or other forms of marginalization.

From a feminist perspective, society used witch-hunts to control and suppress women's autonomy and influence. This interpretation rests on the understanding that the witch-hunts served as a tool for maintaining patriarchal dominance, subjugating women, and reinforcing societal norms that restricted their place and participation.

Modern feminist discourse has reclaimed the figure of the witch as a symbol of resistance and empowerment. The book by Lindy West, The Witches Are Coming, has popularized the use of the word "witch" as a metaphor. One for women defying societal expectations and reclaiming the term "witch" as a badge of honor.

Historically, witch-hunts show how fear and prejudice served as weapons against marginalized groups. Thus, highlighting the need for ongoing critical examination and analysis of these phenomena today.

The principle of "innocent until proven guilty" is now the foundation of many legal systems. This contrasts sharply with the presumption of guilt that characterized the witch-hunts. This principle emerged, in part, as a reaction to the injustices of earlier periods.

The widespread use of torture to extract confessions during witch trials highlights the dangers of coercive interrogation. Modern prohibitions on torture, enshrined in international law, reflect lessons learned from the abuses of the witch-hunt era. The requirement for concrete, verifiable evidence in modern trials owes much to the Enlightenment-era critiques of witchcraft accusations. These standards help to prevent the kinds of arbitrary and baseless prosecutions that defined the witch-hunts.

The legacy of the witch-hunts is a complex and multifaceted one, encompassing a range of cautionary lessons, cultural symbols, and ongoing parallels to modern society. These events serve as a stark reminder of the devastating consequences of fear and prejudice, as well as the importance of reason, justice, and human rights. By studying them, we gain valuable insight not only into the past but also into the enduring challenges of navigating fear, power, and social change in the modern world.

Unchecked fear and societal anxieties, left unaddressed, starkly illustrate the dangers and devastating consequences of the witch-hunts. The widespread persecution of individuals accused of witchcraft was often based on flimsy evidence or mere suspicion. This serves as a chilling reminder of the importance of upholding due process and protecting the rights of the accused. The witch-hunts highlight the need for critical thinking and the importance of separating fact from fiction. Previously, the reliance on superstition and hearsay led to the execution of thousands of innocent people.

The legacy of the witch-hunts also extends to the cultural realm, where the figure of the witch has become a powerful symbol of resistance and empowerment. From the feminist movement's reclaiming of the witch as a symbol of women's power and agency to the use of the witch as a metaphor for social change and activism, the cultural significance of the witch-hunts continues to evolve and adapt. They have inspired a range of artistic and literary works, from Shakespeare's *Macbeth* to Arthur Miller's *The Crucible*. With paintings like Hans Baldung Grien's, *The Witches* continue to captivate audiences and inspire new generations of artists and writers.

In contrast, contemporary art often seeks to humanize the victims of the witch-hunts or reinterpret witches as symbols of female empowerment. Artists like Judy Chicago and Paula Rego have created works that reclaim the narrative, emphasizing the strength and resilience of the accused.

Besides their cultural significance, the witch-hunts also offer valuable lessons for modern society. The persecution of marginalized groups, including women, minorities, and LGBTQ+ individuals, continues to be a pressing concern in the present day. By studying the witch-hunts, we can gain a deeper understanding of how fear and prejudice was used to justify violence and persecution. Society can learn from this and develop strategies for promoting greater tolerance, acceptance, and understanding.

Ultimately, the legacy of the witch-hunts serves as a powerful reminder of the importance of critical thinking, empathy, and human rights in navigating the complexities of modern society. By studying this dark chapter in human history, we can gain a deeper understanding of the enduring challenges of fear, power, and social change. Now we can work towards creating a more just and fairer world for all.

EPILOGUE

The witch-hunts of history stand as stark reminders of the devastating consequences of fear and ignorance. From the torture chambers of Kramer and Sprenger to the chilling trials. Trials led by such figures as Matthew Hopkins and Georg Scherer, this dark chapter of humanity reveals how hysteria can turn neighbor against neighbor, unraveling the very fabric of society. For centuries, powerful figures like these stripped individuals of their dignity and coerced confessions from them. They condemned them for crimes as intangible as the rustling of the wind or the flicker of a shadow. Their only offense was to exist in a time and place where suspicion was a death sentence.

Yet, even in the face of such atrocities, there lies an enduring legacy of resilience. Among the tens of thousands who faced persecution, many went to their deaths proclaiming their innocence. Others, though broken in body, kept a spark of defiance, refusing to cower before the machinery of fear. These stories, tragic as they are, remind us of the profound strength of the human spirit even in the darkest of times.

The lessons of the witch-hunts are just not confined to history. The same mechanisms that fueled them, unquestioned authority, scapegoating, and the manipulation of public fears, resurface in modern forms. Whether it is the ostracization of marginalized communities, the spread of misinformation, or the persecution of those deemed "other," the echoes of these past injustices persist. The witch-hunts compel us to examine our own societies: Where do we allow fear to erode reason? Where do we permit ignorance to override compassion?

Yet there is hope for us as a civilization. To study the witch-hunts is not only to mourn the victims but to illuminate the paths toward understanding, empathy, and justice. By remembering their stories, we honor their lives and affirm our commitment to preventing such horrors from recurring. We recognize the necessity of questioning authority, challenging prejudice, and upholding the principles of fairness and humanity in all aspects of life.

As we close this journey into the past, let us remember those lost, not just as witches, but as mothers, fathers, daughters, sons, and friends. Let their memory serve as a beacon, guiding us toward a future where no one suffers from being different, vulnerable, or misunderstood. Let us transform the shadows of fear into the light of knowledge, ensuring that such darkness never again finds a foothold in our world.

BIBLIOGRAPHY

- *The Discovery of Witches* by Matthew Hopkins, 1647, 2020
- *Daemonologie* by King James VI of Scotland (later James I of England) (2020 reprint)
- *Saducismus Triumphatus* by Joseph Glanvill, 1966
- *Histoire admirable de la possession d'une penitente* by Sebastian Michaelis (English) (digitized version 2011)
- *Witch, Warlock,, and Magician: Historical Sketches of Magic and Witchcraft in England* by W.H. Davenport, 1889
- *Witchcraft, Magic, and Culture, 1736-1951* by Owen Davies, 1999
- *Witches and Neighbors: The Social and Cultural Context of European Witchcraft* by Robin Briggs, 1998
- *Europe's Inner Demons* by Norman Cohn, 1993
- *Witchcraft in Early Modern Scotland: James VI's Demonology and the North Berwick Witches* by Lawrence Normand and Gareth Roberts, 2014
- *Inquisition and Power: Catharism and the Confessing Subject in Medieval Languedoc* by John H. Arnold, 2001
- *The media representation of the crime of witchcraft in early modern Germany: an examination of non-periodical news-sheets and pamphlets, 1533-1669.* By Abaigéal Warfield (Thesis Paper)
- *Witchcraft: A Very Short Introduction* by Malcolm Gaskill, 2010
- *The European Witch-Hunt* by Julian Goodare, 2016
- *Witch-Hunting in Scotland: Law, Politics and Religion* by Brian P. Levack, 2019
- *Witchcraft and Magic in Europe, Volume 4: The Period of the Witch Trials* by Bengt Ankarloo and Stuart Clark, 2002
- *Witches, Midwives, and Nurses: A History of Women Healers* by Barbara Ehrenreich and Deirdre English, 1973
- Witchcraft and the Papacy: An Account Drawing on the Formerly Secret Records of the Roman Inquisition (Studies in Early Modern German History) by Rainer Decker (Author), H. C. Erik Midelfort (Translator), 2008
- Kramer, Heinrich, and Jacob Sprenger. *Malleus Maleficarum.* 1487.

BIBLIOGRAPHY

- The Holy Bible, King James Version. Relevant passages (e.g., Exodus 22:18, Deuteronomy 18:10-12).
- The Code of Hammurabi. Circa 1754 BCE.
- Pope Innocent VIII. *Summis desiderantes affectibus*. 1484.
- Barstow, Anne Llewellyn. *Witchcraze: A New History of the European Witch Hunts*. 1994.
- Briggs, Robin. *Witches and Neighbors: The Social and Cultural Context of European Witchcraft*. 1996.
- Gaskill, Malcolm. *Witchfinders: A Seventeenth-Century English Tragedy*. Harvard 2005.
- Levack, Brian P. *The Witch-Hunt in Early Modern Europe*. Routledge, 2006.
- Midelfort, H. C. Erik. *Witch Hunting in Southwestern Germany 1562–1684: The Social and Intellectual Foundations*. 1972.
- Demos, John. *Entertaining Satan: Witchcraft and the Culture of Early New England*. 1982.
- Hutton, Ronald. *The Witch: A History of Fear, from Ancient Times to the Present*. 2017.
- Monter, E. William. *European Witchcraft*. 1969.
- Purkiss, Diane. *The Witch in History: Early Modern and Twentieth-Century Representations*. 1996.
- Sharpe, James. *Instruments of Darkness: Witchcraft in Early Modern England*. 1996.
- Almond, Philip C. *England's First Demonologist: Reginald Scot and "The Discoverie of Witchcraft"*. 2011.
- Gibbons, Jenny. *Recent Developments in the Study of The Great European Witch Hunt*. 1998.
- Clark, Stuart. *Thinking with Demons: The Idea of Witchcraft in Early Modern Europe*. 1997.
- Maxwell-Stuart, P.G. *Witchcraft: A History*. 2000.
- Oldridge, Darren, ed. *The Witchcraft Reader*. 2002.
- Boyer, Paul, and Stephen Nissenbaum. *Salem Possessed: The Social Origins of Witchcraft*. 1974.
- Behringer, Wolfgang. *Witchcraft Persecutions in Bavaria: Popular Magic, Religious Zealotry and Reason of State in Early Modern Europe*. 1997.
- Burns, William E. *Witch Hunts in Europe and America: An Encyclopedia*. 2003.

About the Author

Dr. W.J. (Bill) Brendle has spent a lifetime pursuing the mysteries that refuse ordinary explanations. A paranormal scholar and historian of the unseen, his fascination with cryptids, witchcraft, and what he calls "realms of high strangeness" began in childhood after personal encounters that defied rational understanding. That spark grew into a lifelong drive to seek answers, test experiences, and study the forces that shape human belief.

Brendle holds a Ph.D. in Metaphysical Humanistic Science with a specialization in parapsychology. He is a cryptozoologist, paranormal investigator, and practicing folk-magick witch. His path has also made him an accomplished outdoorsman — a perspective that deepens his research into cryptids and the landscapes where such legends are said to roam. As a member of the Ancient Free & Accepted Masons and a long-time student of occult traditions, he has studied and practiced disciplines ranging from Tarot and scrying to esoteric Masonry and ceremonial magick.

This breadth of experience allows him to approach the unexplained with both lived practice and historical research, offering readers a unique perspective on folklore, witchcraft, UFO phenomena, and other intersections of culture and mystery.

He is the author of *The Cryptids & Monsters of North Carolina*. He is also the writer, producer, and co-host of the *4 Ever Paranormal* podcast, where stories of the strange are brought to life with atmosphere, scholarship, and an eye toward truth.

Also by W.J. Brendle Ph.D.

www.ingramcontent.com/pod-product-compliance
Lightning Source LLC
LaVergne TN
LVHW041249080426
835510LV00009B/651